59372083666662   FIG

USA TODAY
A GANNETT COMPANY

Lifeline
BIOGRAPHIES

ALEX RODRIGUEZ
Hot Corner, Hot Shot

by Serena Kappes

Twenty-First Century Books · Minneapolis

To David—living with you is like hitting a home run every day.

Twenty-First Century Books
A division of Lerner Publishing Group, Inc.
241 First Avenue North
Minneapolis, MN 55401 U.S.A.

Website address: www.lernerbooks.com

Library of Congress Cataloging-in-Publication Data

Kappes, Serena.
    Alex Rodriguez : hot corner, hot shot / by Serena Kappes.
        p.   cm. — (USA today lifeline biographies)
    Includes bibliographical references and index.
    ISBN 978-0-7613-8155-6 (lib. bdg. : alk. paper)
    1. Rodriguez, Alex, 1975– —Juvenile literature. 2. Baseball players—United States—
Biography—Juvenile literature. I. Title.
GV865.R62K37 2012
796.357'092—dc23 [B]   2011021266

Manufactured in the United States of America
1 – PP – 12/31/11

USA TODAY.
A GANNETT COMPANY

Lifeline
BIOGRAPHIES

USA TODAY
A GANNETT COMPANY

INTRODUCTION

Home run hitter: Alex cheers after seeing his 400th career home run sail into the stands on June 8, 2005.

Historic Home Run

On June 8, 2005, Alex Rodriguez—nicknamed A-Rod—and the New York Yankees faced the Milwaukee Brewers. The Yankees had lost nine of their last 10 games, but A-Rod had a plan to break his team's losing streak and lift their spirits. The third baseman, who was in his second season with the New York Yankees, was two home runs away from making history.

A-Rod had become known as a home run hitter. Back in 1996, his first full season in Major League Baseball (MLB), he hit 36 homers for the Seattle Mariners. In 2002 he slammed an amazing 57 home runs with the Texas Rangers. His home run production went back down to 36 in 2004, but by 2005, he was on track to hit his 400th career home run. The fans at Milwaukee's Miller Park may not have been cheering for the Yankees, but they were excited to see Alex reach that important milestone.

A-Rod started off strong, turning a pitch from left-hander Chris Capuano into his 399th career home run in the first inning. The round-tripper gave the Yanks two runs and an early lead. During his eighth-inning at bat, A-Rod could practically taste victory. The Yankees had a 10–3 lead, but he was aiming for another run.

Alex steadied himself at the plate as he faced relief pitcher Jorge de la Rosa. The slugger got into his batting stance and waited for the pitch. The ball streaked toward him. Swing... connect... the ball was out of there! A-Rod had just slugged his 400th homer! As he rounded the bases, he knew he'd made history. At 29 years old, he was the youngest major leaguer to reach the 400 home run mark.

Team support: Alex is congratulated by his teammates on his 400th career home run, (*from left*) Jorge Posada, Alex, Derek Jeter, and Gary Sheffield.

Ken Griffey Jr., the next youngest, had scored 400 career homers at the age of 30 back in 2000.

To top off A-Rod's big day, the Yankees beat the Brewers with a final score of 12–3. Their losing streak had come to a dramatic end. After the game, Alex had time to think about his accomplishment. He was only the 39th member of the 400 home run club. "It's a special number," A-Rod told reporters. "It was a very special day for me, especially if you do it in a win that we needed most desperately."

No one was prouder than Yankees manager Joe Torre. He had shaken up his players by canceling their regular batting practice earlier that day. Some reporters joked that the tactic had worked so well, he should cancel batting practice more often. Torre was grateful for A-Rod's role in the team's victory, and he was confident that A-Rod would continue to achieve great things in the future. "The shape he's in, the way he works—who knows where he's going?" Torre said. That's a question many ask about one of baseball's brightest stars.

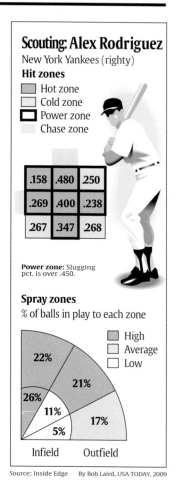

Scouting: Alex Rodriguez
New York Yankees (righty)

Hit zones
- Hot zone
- Cold zone
- Power zone
- Chase zone

.158	.480	.250
.269	.400	.238
.267	.347	.268

Power zone: Slugging pct. is over .450.

Spray zones
% of balls in play to each zone
- High
- Average
- Low

22%
21%
26%
11%
17%
5%

Infield   Outfield

Source: Inside Edge   By Bob Laird, USA TODAY, 2009

Hometown: Alex Rodriguez was born in New York City. This photo of the city was taken in 1975, the year Alex was born.

Born for Baseball

Alexander Emmanuel Rodriguez was born on July 27, 1975. He lived with his family in the Washington Heights section of Manhattan, part of New York City. His parents, Lourdes Navarro Rodriguez and Victor Rodriguez, were immigrants from the Dominican Republic, a Spanish-speaking island nation between Cuba and Puerto Rico. They had come to the United States to find good jobs. Victor opened a shoe store, and Lourdes took a job on an assembly line at General Motors. At home Lourdes and Victor spoke both English and Spanish. When baby Alex was born, he already had an older sister, Susy, and an older brother, Joe.

Even as a two-year-old, Alex showed an interest in baseball. He carried around a red plastic bat and swung at everything he could, sometimes even breaking household items. To practice his throwing, he would bounce a small rubber ball against a wall for hours on end. That was just fine with Alex's dad, who once had been a catcher with a Dominican baseball league. Victor loved that his youngest child had such an interest in the sport.

"When Alex was little, all he wanted me to do was throw him Wiffle balls that he'd hit with a plastic bat. He had that drive from the beginning."

—Joe Rodriguez, Alex's brother

Victor dreamed of returning to the Dominican Republic one day, and he finally got his chance. By the time Alex was four, Victor had been able to save enough money from his shoe store to move his family back to the island. The Rodriguezes bought a beautiful four-bedroom home one block from the beach in Santo Domingo, the Dominican Republic's capital. Victor still owned his thriving shoe store. His New York relatives worked there and sent some of the profits to the Rodriguezes.

Family Support

The year-round warm weather in the Dominican Republic was perfect for practicing baseball. The island already had contributed a number of major league baseball stars. Juan Marichal, a Hall of Fame pitcher who played in the 1950s and 1960s; home run star Sammy Sosa; Boston Red Sox left fielder Manny Ramirez; and New York Mets pitcher Pedro Martinez all had come from the Dominican Republic.

By the time he was six, Alex had improved so much that he was playing with boys three and four years older than he was. One day Alex went to the local park to join some friends for a game. As his parents watched, Alex walked with a yellow bat over to a makeshift home plate. As the ball approached, he put all his power into his swing. The ball soared into the air, past the third baseman,

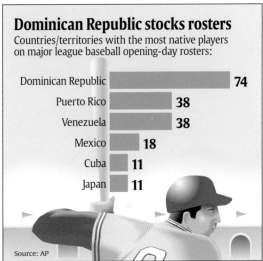

USA TODAY Snapshots®

Dominican Republic stocks rosters
Countries/territories with the most native players on major league baseball opening-day rosters:

Dominican Republic	74
Puerto Rico	38
Venezuela	38
Mexico	18
Cuba	11
Japan	11

Source: AP

By Ellen J. Horrow and Frank Pompa, USA TODAY, 2003

In the sandlot: Alex spent many hours in Santo Domingo playing baseball at a field like this one.

and landed in a faraway corner of the field. As Alex began rounding the bases, an outfielder scooped up the ball and threw it to the shortstop, who rocketed it to home plate. But he was too late—Alex had gotten there before the ball arrived. He had scored his first-ever home run!

Everyone cheered, especially his parents and his teammates. But no one was more thrilled than Alex. "I was almost crying, I was so happy," he later recalled.

It was no surprise to his mother that Alex had developed such skill. "He was just very focused from the time he was a child and just wasn't interested in anything else," she recalled. "He didn't care about the sun or the rain. He just had to play ball and would cry if I didn't take him to the park every day."

Usually the youngest kid on the team, Alex started out playing second base. He hated to lose. "If I lost, I would go home crying angry tears," he later wrote. "The whole night I would think of ways we could win the next day."

Back in the USA

When Alex was eight, life changed drastically. His family's shoe store in New York wasn't doing well financially. The Rodriguezes were forced to sell their dream home and leave island living behind. They returned to the United States, where they hoped they could find more financial opportunities than they had in the Dominican Republic.

This time they chose Kendall, Florida, a suburb of Miami. There Victor opened a new shoe store, and Alex tried to adjust to his new life. In the Dominican Republic, he had gotten used to speaking only Spanish in school and with friends and relatives. But at his new school in Florida, everyone spoke English. "My transition from speaking all Spanish in the Dominican Republic to English-based fourth grade proved rocky," Alex later wrote. The adjustment was difficult for Alex, and he had a tough time in school.

Luckily, Alex had a much easier time on the sports field. Soon after moving to Kendall, he went to a nearby park to check out practice

IN FOCUS

Renaissance Man

As a boy, Alex admired Leonardo da Vinci, a 15th-century artist, scientist, mathematician, and writer. Alex first learned about Leonardo when Lourdes put a print of the *Mona Lisa*, the artist's most famous painting, in his room. Alex liked Leonardo because he was a man of many talents.

of a local youth league baseball team. Every day for a month, he sat and watched. Then one day, the team's catcher didn't show up. So the coach, Juan Diego Arteaga, called over to Alex and asked him if he wanted to join in.

That was the start of his baseball career in Kendall. Coach Arteaga became like a second father to Alex. The coach's son, J. D., became Alex's best friend.

Alex would soon need their emotional support. His father was again struggling financially. The Miami shoe store was failing. One day, when Alex was nine, his dad told the family he was going to New York for a short time to try to find some work. He never came home.

"I knew he'd come back as surely as the sun would rise on the Sunshine State," Alex later wrote. "He had been a great dad. He played catch with me. He taught me math. He loved me. But each passing week dug deeper a grave of pain. Finally, my hope dried up and died. I gave up."

As painful as it was for young Alex, his mom and siblings rallied around him and showered him with love and affection. To support her children, Lourdes took on two jobs—working in a Miami immigration office during the day and as a waitress at night. While she was at work, Alex's sister, Susy, was the "secretary of education" and helped Alex with his homework, while brother Joe was the "secretary of sports" and coached him on his baseball skills.

The Arteagas also took Alex under their wing. When they'd go to see local baseball games, they'd bring him along. And when Arteaga bought his son sports equipment, he also purchased some for Alex. "He was the father I didn't have," Alex recalled. "Everything he gave to his son, he gave to me."

Arteaga took the boys to the Hank Kline Club of the Boys & Girls Clubs of Miami-Dade, which had the area's best baseball teams. It was a place where Alex could play his favorite sport and also find a sense of community, something he desperately needed. Instead of staying home after school, he had somewhere to go that made him feel good about himself.

Learning the Game

At the Hank Kline Club, Alex met another influential figure in his life, Eddy Rodriguez (no relation to Alex's family), who worked as a coach there. Rodriguez had played minor-league baseball. At the club, he had even coached future major leaguers such as Jose Canseco, Rafael Palmeiro, and Alex Fernandez. Alex dreamed of joining those guys in the big leagues one day. "Believe in yourself," Rodriguez told Alex. "But ask more of yourself. This will sustain you in times both good and bad."

By then Alex was also a serious student who consistently earned good grades. He later admitted that unlike a lot of kids his age, he liked homework.

His baseball hero was Baltimore Orioles shortstop Cal Ripken Jr. Ripken was six foot four, bigger than most shortstops but just as agile as smaller players. He was also a great hitter. But it wasn't only Ripken's skills on the field that impressed Alex. Ripken was also a role model who always signed autographs for his fans. He had such a strong work ethic that he never missed a game. In fact, he went on to set the all-time record for playing the most games in a row—2,632. That's exactly the kind of player Alex wanted to be.

IN F⊙CUS

Cal Ripken Jr.

Cal Ripken Jr., nicknamed the Iron Man, played his first major-league baseball game in 1981 for the Baltimore Orioles. He played for the Orioles—first at shortstop, later at third base—for the next 20 years. For much of his career he was coached by his father, Cal Ripken Sr. From 1987 to 1992, Cal's brother Billy Ripken also played for the Orioles. Cal Ripken Jr. holds the record for most career home runs by a shortstop, with 345. He also hit 57 homers as a third baseman, bringing his total to 402.

Role model: Cal Ripken Jr. was a hard-working shortstop who set the record for games played in a row (2,632).

And Alex was doing everything he could to get there. In 1986, when Alex was 11, his Hank Kline Club team won the Pony League baseball championship, a national competition for young players. A year later, Alex played shortstop with the club's traveling team, which went to tournaments throughout the southeastern United States. With Alex on board, the squad won two national championships and three city championships. He was even awarded the league batting title one year for having the highest batting average in the league.

Alex was dedicated. While the other boys joked around by the hotel pool after road games, he sat in his room and watched sports

Ripken sees no need to sit down

From the Pages of USA TODAY

Like seconds in a minute and days in a week, Cal Ripken just keeps going. And going and going and going.

No active major league player has stayed more active than Ripken. The Baltimore Orioles' slick-fielding shortstop has played in 1,302 consecutive games.

"To play that long without having a serious injury is an accomplishment in itself," says Carlton Fisk, the 18-year veteran catcher for the Chicago White Sox. "That's probably the key to the streak. An injury can happen at any time, in the most freakish moments. He's been able to stay away from that, so that's amazing."

Baseball's all-time consecutive-game record of 2,130 belongs to the late Lou Gehrig. It's a record—like Babe Ruth's home runs and Ty Cobb's stolen bases—that people said would never be broken (until Hank Aaron and Lou Brock proved otherwise).

news on ESPN, studying the pro players' moves. In the morning, Alex did exercises—100 sit-ups and 100 push-ups. He was also the only player on his team who could hit fastballs.

Although Alex loved baseball, the summer before eighth grade, he felt as if he was burning out on the sport. He sat down with his mom and told her how he felt. She didn't want Alex to waste his talent and convinced him to try one more season at the sport.

Alex attended a new school for eighth grade and then went to Christopher Columbus Catholic High School for ninth grade. There he

Don't count out Ripken. He has played in every game the last seven seasons and Sunday will tie Everett Scott for second place on the consecutive-game list. Ripken, who began his streak May 30, 1982, as a rookie, needs five more seasons of luck and perseverance to reach Gehrig's record. But it was not his plan to go this long without a rest.

"To take a day off, maybe it would help me statistically or selfishly, but it seems like it's against everything I've worked towards," says Ripken, battling the most prolonged batting slump of his nine-year career.

"As (Atlanta's) Dale Murphy said when he had his streak, he didn't set out to do it. He just wanted to remain healthy and go out and do his job every day. . . . That's how it is with me."

Ripken is batting .209 (40-for-191) with seven home runs and 28 RBI. He finished cold last season, hitting .198 in September and October.

Murphy's streak of 740 games ended when he took a day off July 9, 1986. When Ripken finally sits down, which some have suggested, it likely won't be by his choosing.

"I've always been one to be active and not one to watch the action on the sidelines," he says. "If I was playing basketball, I felt I didn't need a rest. If I was playing soccer, I didn't need to come out. That feeling just carried over into baseball."

Not that Ripken, 29, hasn't considered taking a break.

"There have been a few times when I thought it would have been easier if I said, 'I don't want to play today,' " he says. "Some of those days have been the best of my career."

—Chuck Johnson

played varsity basketball and baseball. But despite his advanced level of play, Alex wasn't the school's starting shortstop. He served as backup to an older player. His coach told him, "We have a shortstop the next two years. Maybe as a senior you'll get an opportunity to play."

But that wasn't good enough for Alex. He wanted to use the baseball skills he'd worked so hard to hone. His mom agreed that he should find a school where his special athletic gifts wouldn't be wasted. The situation "motivated me to work harder and forced me to look elsewhere," Alex later wrote. The school he found was Westminster Christian High School.

USA TODAY
A GANNETT COMPANY

CHAPTER TWO

Fierce competitor: Alex's focus on baseball was clear throughout high school, when he played for the Westminster Warriors.

Field of Dreams

Alex's best friend, J. D. Arteaga, was already attending Westminster, a private school in nearby Fort Lauderdale, Florida. Westminster was known for its strong academic and athletic programs. Alex really wanted to go there, but he faced a major roadblock: his mom couldn't afford the $5,000 yearly tuition. Yet Lourdes felt that Westminster was the right place to help shape Alex as a person, a student, and an athlete. She liked the school's religious classes, tough academics, and emphasis on educating teens to be well-rounded adults. The school seemed like the best spot for her bright, talented son.

Lourdes sat Alex down and told him her plan. If Westminster accepted him for his sophomore year, she would put in more hours of work to make extra money. The family would also apply for financial aid (money from the school) to cover the remaining costs.

At the end of his freshman year at Christopher Columbus Catholic High School, Alex applied to and was accepted at Westminster. He was thrilled. Not only was he joining J. D., he would also be going to a school where many baseball players went on to top-level college teams and the pros. The Westminster Warriors, led by Coach Rich Hofman, was one of the best high school baseball teams in the country. In 1990 the Warriors had won the state baseball championship and had finished 10th in *USA Today*'s national ranking of high school baseball teams.

Tragedy

At Westminster, Alex fell easily into campus life. The handsome, green-eyed teen was popular and a good student. "I took school seriously," Alex later wrote. "I made the honor roll and stayed out of trouble, playing all three major sports [baseball, basketball, and football]."

But during football season of his sophomore year, when Alex was 15, he experienced a heartbreaking event. Juan Diego Arteaga was in the stands watching a game when he suffered a heart attack and collapsed. Soon after, he died. "I felt someone had torn my heart out and smashed it," Alex wrote. "J. D. and I grew closer, as brothers. We shared each other's loss, although we really didn't talk about it much. We gave each other strength."

"The ripples of his kindness reached many people. He treated me as a son, and I miss him as a father."

—Alex on Juan Diego Arteaga, his first coach and mentor

Alex was determined to succeed—and to make Arteaga proud of him. "I started trying to lead by example and never missed a day of school and always did my homework," Alex remembers.

In the spring, Alex hit the baseball field for practice. Coach Hofman didn't exactly see a future MVP when he first met the lean and lanky player. "Alex wasn't Superman. He was a tall, thin, not very strong kid," Hofman recalled. "But he did have real nice actions [on the field]. That helped him defensively, but he was not yet a polished hitter."

During the district finals, the team faced off against Gulliver Preparatory School, one of its biggest rivals. In the first inning, Alex came to bat with a runner on base. Omar Fernandez, Gulliver's senior star pitcher, wasn't intimidated by the sophomore batter. He delivered a fastball. As the ball came toward Alex, he swung with all his might. The ball rocketed over the fence in what the *Miami Herald* called "a two-run monster that rainbowed its way over the 375-foot sign in left-center."

Alex's homer helped lead the team to a 10–0 victory against one of its fiercest competitors. Ultimately, though, the Warriors didn't make it to the state championships. It wasn't a star-making season for Alex either—he ended with a .256 batting average (just over 2.5 hits for every 10 at bats—a little more than 25 percent), the lowest average he'd had in his baseball career to that point. But he'd learned a lot and was ready for the next year.

Two-Sport Star

After the season ended, Alex was determined to get stronger. One day Coach Hofman approached him in the weight room. "Well, tenth grade, you had an OK year. Next year everyone will get to know you, and in twelfth grade you'll be the number one pick in the country," Hofman told Alex. Hofman wanted to boost Alex's morale. He thought that if Alex kept working hard, by his senior year, he could be the first high school baseball player chosen by a professional team during the major-league draft.

At the age of 16, when Alex returned to school in the fall of his junior year, he was stronger. He even played quarterback on the Westminster football team. He was picked as an all-state quarterback and led his team to a 9–1 record. College football scouts began showing up at games and calling him one of the best quarterbacks in the state.

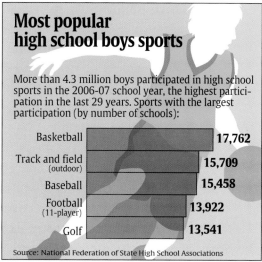

USA TODAY Snapshots®

Most popular high school boys sports

More than 4.3 million boys participated in high school sports in the 2006-07 school year, the highest participation in the last 29 years. Sports with the largest participation (by number of schools):

Basketball	17,762
Track and field (outdoor)	15,709
Baseball	15,458
Football (11-player)	13,922
Golf	13,541

Source: National Federation of State High School Associations

By Ellen J. Horrow and Sam Ward, USA TODAY, 2007

Taking the snap: Alex prepares to throw the ball as quarterback of the Westminster high school football team in 1991.

By the time Alex arrived for the first practice of the baseball season, Coach Hofman saw a very different player. Alex had shot up two inches (5.08 centimeters) and had added 30 pounds (13.6 kilograms) of muscle to his frame. He was now six foot two (1.88 meters) and weighed 185 pounds (83.9 kg). But the extra bulk didn't slow him down. In fact, he was quicker than he had been in his sophomore year, and his reflexes were even keener on the field. "I could bench-press 310 pounds (140.6 kg) and hit the ball 400 feet," Alex later wrote.

On the field, other teams soon noticed that Alex was a far-improved player. As the season progressed, opposing pitchers became intimidated by his powerful batting. Rather than throw him fastballs, they used slower pitches, such as curveballs, to throw off his timing. Alex was also a fast runner and soon became a talented base stealer.

Impact: Alex's offseason practice improved his skills. He helped his team win the Florida state championship during his junior season in 1991.

By the regular season's end, the Warriors had a 33–2 record. They sailed into the state tournament and made it to the finals against Florida Air Academy. With Alex as leadoff batter and J. D. Arteaga as pitcher, the team won the game and became the state AA (small high school) champions. *USA Today* named Westminster the number one high school team in the country, and Alex was one of eight Westminster players named to the all-state team. He also earned all-America honors, awarded to the top high school athletes in the country, with his .477 batting average, 42 stolen bases, 6 home runs, and 52 runs scored.

June 24, 1992

Florida coach wins baseball honor, team tops high school poll

From the Pages of USA TODAY

Miami Westminster Christian's Rich Hofman caps his 25th year of coaching with his fourth state championship and this year's USA TODAY high school baseball coach of the year award.

``I can't ever remember wanting to do something else," said Hofman, whose coaching career began in 1967 for $4,850 a year. ``I'm very thankful to the Lord and give Him all the credit."

He is the first of this season's USA TODAY high school baseball honorees. The player of the year and all-USA team will be announced Thursday.

Hofman, president of the new Baseball Coaches Association of America, is 540-163 in 24 years with four state titles one second and two third-place finishes. Forty-one graduates have played college baseball—23 on scholarship—and eight have gone pro.

His program has had an uphill climb.

Consider the 1969 season, his second year at the school and its first baseball team: Hofman's first team went 2-13 with only one extra-base hit.

With time came improvement:

- Westminster finished the 1970 season 9-7 and in 1974 had its first 20- win season.
- In 1977, it produced its first scholarship player, pitcher Bud Gray, who went to the University of Georgia.
- In 1981 came the first of four state titles (Class 1A and 2A). ``That was my greatest thrill until this year," Hofman said. ``I hadn't even visited a state tourney until then."
- In 1989, he was named national coach of the year by the American Baseball Coaches Association.

This year, Westminster finished 33-2 and is top-ranked in the USA, going into next week's final poll. It's the first time a school from a lower division has been ranked No. 1. Westminster has 280 students in four grades.

—Dave Krider

Alex began hearing talk about his chances of being recruited to the major leagues, and it made him a little nervous. "I was just a kid, and scouts were talking about what would happen in two or three years. That's an awful lot of pressure to be under," he said.

But he refused to be intimidated. He wanted to focus on reaching his potential as an athlete. His senior-year football season, however, wasn't quite as impressive as his junior year. One day, while tackling during a kickoff, Alex injured his wrist. Everyone—including Alex himself—worried that he had destroyed his chances to play baseball in the spring. The injury turned out to be just a hairline fracture, but it was

Being a teen: Alex *(right)* goofs around with a friend during his high school years.

enough to convince him to give up playing basketball to stay strong for the baseball season.

Although he had good friends in school—including J. D.—teenage Alex did little besides homework and sports. During his winter break, instead of relaxing, he played in the Arizona Instructional League, a major-league–sponsored program in which young players work on their games alongside older players.

Hitting the books: Alex was a good student in high school. Between studying and baseball, he didn't have time for much else.

"Setbacks and tribulations never stopped Alex from pursuing his dream. It didn't matter what happened around us, he was always focused on his goal."

—Lourdes Navarro, Alex's mom

In Arizona being around more experienced players taught Alex about teamwork and made him realize how passionate he was about baseball. For the rest of his senior year, his focus was going to be entirely on the sport.

On the ball: Alex was under a lot of pressure during his senior baseball season at Westminster in 1993.

Senior Sensation

In 1993, when Alex's senior-year baseball season began, he was in top form. The magazine *Baseball America*, which covers high school and college baseball, named him the number one high school prospect in the country. One college coach described Alex by saying, "If you were to sit in front of a computer and say, 'How would I construct the perfect shortstop?'

you'd put all the data in, and then you would see Alex Rodriguez."

That kind of praise made Alex feel good, but it was also a lot of pressure to live up to. And when Alex hit the field for his first game that spring, he could hardly believe his eyes: sitting in the stands were 68 pro and college scouts with notebooks, stopwatches, and radar guns in their hands. They all took notes about Alex. When he ran to first base, they clocked his speed. When he threw the ball, they aimed their radar guns to measure his throws.

After the game, Alex went home and told his mother about all the hoopla. She had sound words of advice for her son: "The scouts are there because they have already seen something they like. So don't change. Just be yourself."

By the season's end, the team had lost only four games. Once again, they entered the state tournament. This time, they faced Cardinal Newman High School. In the ninth inning, an opposing batter hit a routine ground ball. Alex picked it up but threw too hard, past first base and down the right-field line. Alex's mistake cost the team the game. They were out of the running for the championship.

Luckily, Coach Hofman didn't blame Alex for the loss. He understood that even the best players make mistakes from time to time. "Those plays he [usually] does with his eyes closed," said Hofman. "He's meant so much to this team. He's done so much. You can't fault him. He's human."

And Alex certainly didn't suffer much from his error on the field. He finished his season with a .419 average (124 hits in 296 at bats), 17 homers, 70 RBIs, and 90 stolen bases in 100 games. He was also named the USA Baseball Junior Player of the Year and was a finalist for the Golden Spikes Award, given to the top amateur player in the country. On top of all this, he won the Gatorade National Student-Athlete Award.

Most Wanted

The scouts who'd been watching him all season bombarded Alex with offers. Coach Hofman's prediction seemed to be coming true. He was considered the number one draft pick in the United States. Alex didn't know what to do. Should he accept an offer from a major-league team or do what he'd always planned on doing—going to college?

He needed to talk to someone who'd gone through the same thing. Derek Jeter, who was playing for a New York Yankees' minor-league team at the time, had been the top high school player a year earlier. Derek had dealt with the same choice Alex had to make. "Everyone in the world was giving me advice—teachers, coaches, friends," Alex

The new Yankee: Derek Jeter was drafted by the Yankees in 1992.

IN F⬤CUS

Derek Jeter

Derek Jeter was born on June 26, 1974, making him one year and one month older than Alex Rodriguez. Derek was born in New Jersey but grew up in Kalamazoo, Michigan. Even as a small child, he was a huge fan of the New York Yankees. In his senior year of high school, the Yankees drafted him and he spent the summer of 1992 with the Gulf Coast League Yankees in Tampa, Florida.

recalled. "I decided to call Derek, even though I didn't know him. I figured he knew what I was going through." During the phone call, Derek told Alex to keep his focus on the game and to get professional help in figuring out his future plan.

So while Alex weighed his decision, he signed with a sports agent, Scott Boras, who represented big names in baseball such as Barry Bonds and Bernie Williams. As Boras worked behind the scenes to secure a solid professional contract for his new client, Alex also accepted the scholarship from the University of Miami. That way whatever happened, he had options.

When scouts heard that Alex had accepted the college scholarship, they came clamoring even faster, trying to change his mind. Teams faxed offers to Boras's office. The Seattle Mariners had the first draft

Baseball's agent: Sports agent Scott Boras, shown here in his office in the mid-1990s, helped Alex as he entered the draft in 1993.

For Rodriguez, the end of innocence

From the Pages of
<u>USA TODAY</u>

The innocence of youth is sometimes struck down by some life-altering experience. Yet, for most, the transition to adulthood is gradual, and defining moments only come to light after many years.

Alex Rodriguez, on the other hand, is acutely aware that his life is changing. All he has to do is a pick up a newspaper or telephone. Even before he turned 18 Tuesday, Rodriguez knew he was moving forward at warp speed.

"I'm ready to start a new era," says Rodriguez, the prized high school baseball star from Miami Westminster Christian. "It has been a long 17 years."

But also productive. As he competes this week in the U.S. Olympic Festival, the 6-3, 195-pound shortstop remains at a crossroads. Such is the fate of a sensation— USA TODAY's high school player of the year—picked No. 1 in the June amateur draft by the Seattle Mariners, yet also coveted by the University of Miami (Fla.).

Rodriguez, son of former Dominican "winter ball" catcher Victor Rodriguez,

pick because they had finished last in their division in 1992, so they were most likely to draft Alex. But if Seattle didn't offer Alex a contract, the second pick would go to the Los Angeles Dodgers. Until draft day, it wasn't clear where Alex would end up.

Alex liked the idea of playing in sunny Los Angeles and seeing his family when the Dodgers, part of the National League (NL), played the Florida Marlins in Miami. The Seattle Mariners, on the other hand, were an American League (AL) team and didn't travel to Florida. They also had a long history of losing: their one winning season was in 1991.

says he can foresee postponing a major league playing career and attending Miami. He has accepted an athletic scholarship and, unless the Mariners comply with his contractual requirements, he'll be a Hurricane.

Although Rodriguez contends the Mariners knew of his demands—"I was as serious and honest as a 17-year-old could be"—he is not entirely responsible for the deadlock.

"There were 50 or 60 phone calls over a four-to-five-day period that were not returned after we drafted him," says Mariners spokesman Dave Aust.

At home in Miami, the Rodriguez family has assembled a sort of Team Alex representation group, led by his mother, Lourdes—divorced from Victor—and sister Susy Dunand, an aspiring attorney. Together with "adviser" Scott Boras, an established baseball agent, Team Alex set $2.5 million over three years as a minimum salary. They also seek a so-called big-league contract, like the one given Todd Van Poppel by the Oakland Athletics in 1990, stipulating that a player is not assigned to a minor league team in the franchise's farm club system.

These contractual prerequisites are supposed to compensate for the Mariners being an American League team. Rodriguez says he prefers the National League.

Seattle's response? A three-year, $1 million deal, including $500,000 to sign and the guarantee that Rodriguez will be whisked up from the minors in September when major league rosters expand.

"Baseball is in my blood, but unfortunately money is a part of it," he says. "It kind of takes all of the fun out of it, to tell the truth."

The fun might yet return, but the innocence is lost.

—Steve Woodward

"The past ten years my teams had won eight championships," Alex later wrote. "All I knew was winning."

On June 3, 1993, the day the draft picks were announced, Alex's pal J. D. hosted a party for him. All of Alex's family and friends were there, anxiously awaiting the news. At 1:14 P.M., the phone rang. It was the Mariners. As expected, they wanted Alex on their team.

But Alex wasn't quick to jump at an offer. When a reporter asked if he was going to sign with the Mariners or go to the University of Miami, Alex answered carefully: "I'm not in a rush. It depends on how

Life-changing phone call: Alex listens on June 3, 1993, as the Seattle Mariners ask him to join their team. He is surrounded by his mother *(left)* and many friends.

nice [the Mariners] want to be in negotiations. We just want [a deal] that is fair."

Big Deal

As his agent began negotiating with the Mariners, Alex was named *USA Today*'s national high school player of the year. He also got to participate in the Olympic Festival, run by the U.S. Olympic Committee, which prepares young athletes for international competition. During the festival, Alex traveled to a tournament in San Antonio, Texas. At a game in July, while Alex was in the dugout, a wildly thrown warm-up ball hit him in the side of the face and knocked him out. His cheekbone was broken—but he would be okay.

As Alex healed, negotiations continued between Alex's agent and the Mariners. Boras wanted at least $1 million per year for his client, but the Mariners offered less. University of Miami classes were scheduled to start in late August. According to the rules of professional baseball, if Alex

USA TODAY Snapshots®

Career home runs by No. 1 overall draft picks

Ken Griffey Jr. (1987) **619[1]**
Alex Rodriguez (1993) **562[1]**
Chipper Jones (1990) **416[1]**
Harold Baines (1977) **384**
Darryl Strawberry (1980) **335**

Note: With year drafted; 1 – active
Source: USA TODAY research

By Matt Young and Web Bryant, USA TODAY, 2009

attended classes there, the Mariners would lose their draft rights, and he'd be ineligible for professional play for the next three years.

With the Mariners deal stalled, on August 31, Alex decided to go to school. As he walked through the campus, a scout from the Mariners stopped him before he could go inside one of the buildings. The team was willing to keep negotiating. By 2:00 A.M., Alex and the Mariners had agreed on a record-setting $1.35 million contract.

Soon Alex was sitting at his mother's kitchen table, along with members of the Mariners front office, and signing his name to the contract. What he had dreamed about his entire life had come true. He was going to play professional baseball.

The new guy: Alex signs autographs in Seattle, Washington, during his first batting practice with the Mariners in September 1993.

The Go-Between

■■■■■

Alex had suddenly become a millionaire. But he didn't want to get carried away with foolish purchases. With his agent's help, he set up a budget plan. From his paycheck, he would take $500 in cash and a $500 credit card allowance every month. The rest would go into the bank. Alex allowed himself a few special purchases, though, including a black-and-gold Jeep for himself and a Mercedes-Benz for his mother. Best of all, he paid off the mortgage (money owed) on his mother's house. With this gift, he wanted to thank her for all she'd done for him.

In early September, Alex traveled to Seattle to visit the team and tour the city. His tour guide was Ken Griffey Jr., a 23-year-old batting champion and one of Seattle's most popular players. The two young men instantly hit it off. Griffey understood what Alex had gone through during the drafting process. Griffey had been the first draft pick in 1987 and knew what that kind of pressure was like.

To prepare for the spring season, Alex traveled to Peoria, Arizona. He lived in a dormitory and trained once again with the Arizona Instructional League. Team manager John McNamara quickly got a strong impression of Alex's talent. In his first game, Alex kept five batters from scoring with his lightning-quick fielding. "You couldn't ask for a better-played game of shortstop," McNamara said. "The kid looks and plays mature. He's loaded with talent, all the tools they've been talking about."

Learning from the best: During Alex's first trip to Seattle in 1993, Ken Griffey Jr. *(above)* showed Alex around the city. Griffey was one of the most successful players on the Mariners.

Equally important, Alex got along well with his teammates. When a sporting goods company sent him a huge supply of equipment, he shared it with the other guys.

Following his time in Arizona, Alex headed home to Miami for several months. He wanted to keep up his fitness level. He spent five hours a day lifting weights, running, and fielding.

Pro Ball

Before he knew it, it was late February and time for spring training. Saying good-bye was tough on his mother, Lourdes, who drove her teenage son to the airport. "I wanted to cry," she later said, "but I could not allow myself to do that. I couldn't let him see that I was worried or sad or even scared for him. I was the tree trunk of the family, and the tree trunk cannot fall or else all the branches will go with it."

When Alex arrived at the Mariners' spring training camp in Arizona, he was amazed at the dedication of the other major leaguers. Practice began at 10:00 A.M., but one day, Alex arrived at 7:00 A.M. and a few other players were already there. Training ended at 2:00 P.M. But once Alex forgot his pager and returned at 6:00 P.M. to find batting champ Edgar Martinez practicing his swing in the batting cages. "Those veterans showed me that success in anything begins with dedication and hard work," Alex later wrote.

When spring training was over, the team sent Alex to Appleton, Wisconsin, where he would be playing for the Mariners' Class A minor-league team, the Appleton Foxes of the Midwest League. (The minor leagues are divided into several classes: rookie league is the lowest, followed by Class A, Class AA, and Class AAA.) In Appleton, Alex shared an apartment with a married player and his wife.

After 65 games with Appleton, he had hit .319, with 14 home runs and 55 RBIs. He was chosen to play in the Midwest League's all-star game, but at that point, he had already been promoted to the next minor-league level, the Class AA Jacksonville Suns in the Southern League. During his first game with the team, he scored a home run.

May 26, 1994

Pick pans out: Rodriguez, Seattle's No. 1 in '93, dazzles in Class A

From the Pages of
USA TODAY

One year after he was the first player taken overall in the annual major league draft, Alex Rodriguez is on a fast track to the majors, but it is not a race track.

Rodriguez was a high school shortstop who earned pre-draft ratings that were comparable to those given Ken Griffey Jr., his future teammate in Seattle.

Like Griffey, Rodriguez is crushing the ball. Unlike Griffey, he is doing it in Class A for the Appleton (Wis.) Foxes.

Rodriguez is batting .320 with 12 home runs and 38 RBI in 43 games. "And I don't get too many fastballs," he says.

Mariners general manager Woody Woodward says he's in no hurry to move 18-year-old Rodriguez up.

"He's one year out of high school," says Woodward. "We don't want to move him too quickly. But if he keeps playing the way he has been, we will be looking at a move at some point in the year."

The Mariners are enthused by what they have seen, especially when you consider he has compiled these impressive numbers after a slow start.

"He has played very well offensively, hit with power and done well defensively, too," says Woodward.

He's running well, going 11-for-15 on steals. "I don't know of any part of his game that's lagging," says Woodward.

Rodriguez says the toughest adjustment is playing every day. "You always hear it's a grind," he says. "There is a lot of mental preparation."

He admitted he has had lapses of concentration in the field. "I've made some foolish errors," he says.

Rodriguez is 6–3 [1.92 m], 195 pounds [88.4 kg], fast, agile and powerful. When he makes it, all the short-term considerations will be forgotten.

"He's just what we expected," Woodward says.

—Rod Beaton

Then three weeks later, he was promoted all the way up to the major leagues to join the Mariners for a game in Boston. Alex couldn't believe it. "I stayed up late calling family, friends, and old coaches—'I'm going to the show!'" he told them.

"You get vibes from young players. The kid who is scared sits at the end of the bench. This spring, when I was ready to [bring young players off the bench], Alex always became highly visible. He would grab a bat or his glove. In his own way, he was telling me he was ready."

— Lou Piniella, former Seattle Mariners manager

At only 18, he was the youngest major-league player in 10 years (Jose Rijo had become a New York Yankee at the age of 19 in 1984). Although some members of the Mariners staff thought it was too soon to bring Alex on board, the team's manager, Lou Piniella, fought to bring him there. Piniella felt the Mariners "needed a spark," and he hoped Alex would provide that spark.

Taking His Lumps

On July 8, 1994, Alex started at shortstop against the Boston Red Sox. As Alex headed to the plate for his first at bat, he was incredibly nervous. "My body felt jittery, and my knees buckled. I could barely stand," he later wrote.

After 17 games, Alex was hitting .204. But by August, a more serious problem put an end to Alex's time in the major leagues. The contract between the major-league players and team owners had expired, and the two sides couldn't reach an agreement. The owners shut down the major-league season on August 11. The

IN FOCUS

Big-League Teasing

At his first major-league game with the Mariners, a teammate handed Alex coupons to a fast-food restaurant and joked, "You're making one point three million. When you get sent back down to the minors, take the guys out to lunch down there."

minor-league baseball season, however, was still in full swing.

The Mariners didn't want Alex sitting around during the strike—he needed to keep getting experience. So on August 2, management sent him to the Mariners' Class AAA team in Calgary, Canada, where he ended the season. It was a good choice. The remainder of the major-league season, including the World Series, was canceled that year. Alex looked at his time in Calgary as an opportunity to improve his skills further. When his season there ended, he walked away with a respectable .311 average, 6 home runs, and 21 RBIs.

Instead of going home to Miami, he decided to play in a winter league in the Dominican Republic. Many players from the minor and major leagues go to the challenging winter leagues to keep their skills in tip-top shape.

It was Alex's first time back to the island since he was a little boy. But it proved to be a tough experience. Alex garnered only a .179 batting average and wasn't up to par against his tough competition. "I was overmatched and my mind really wasn't into it," Alex later admitted. "I think [the league] woke me up a little bit. I recommend it to every young player."

In April, Alex started the 1995 season with the minor-league Tacoma Rainiers. But on May 6, he was called up to the major leagues

Alex experienced some good-natured hazing as a rookie. After one game, his Mariners teammates stole his clothes while he was showering. "When I got out of the shower, all my clothes were gone," he recalled. "Instead, [my teammates made me] sign thirty autographs while wearing a silver dress and balancing in high-heeled shoes."

again after another player was injured. He struggled at bat and on May 27 was sent back to Tacoma, Washington. Then 10 days later, with more Mariners injuries, he returned to the majors.

On June 12, during a game against the Kansas City Royals, Alex scored his first major-league home run. It was an unbelievable feeling. Later in the game, he made an impressive defensive play. Although the Mariners lost the game 10–9, Alex still felt good about his role.

Yet three weeks later, he was back in Tacoma and working on hitting curveballs, one of his few weaknesses. He soon returned to the Mariners, only to be sent back down one more time. "I became a human yo-yo going between Tacoma and Seattle," Alex wrote.

Incredible Ride

Being sent down to the minors was eating away at his self-confidence. He didn't know what to do. Alex even considered going back home and attending the University of Miami, where his best friend, J. D. Arteaga, was playing on the college team. But as always, his mom told him to keep working hard. "I'm so thankful Mom talked me out of it," he wrote. "I know now the adversity made me stronger."

Finally, all of his back-and-forth shuttling came to an end. On August 31, Alex was brought up to play with the Mariners for the rest of the 1995 season. Although he was only a backup shortstop to Luis Sojo, the 20-year-old player was thrilled to be part of the excitement. The team made its way to the playoffs for the first time ever and beat the Yankees three games to two in the American League Division Series (ALDS). "It was an awesome experience," Alex told *Sports Illustrated*.

Unfortunately, when the Mariners went up against the Cleveland Indians in the American League Championship Series (ALCS), the Mariners lost four games to two. After the final game, the home fans at the Seattle Kingdome gave their team—whose motto was "Refuse to Lose"—a "thunderous, moving ovation . . . to show their thanks for the season's incredible ride that saved baseball in Seattle," Alex recalled. The exciting postseason gave Seattle fans something to cheer about and a renewed interest in their home team.

IN F⊙CUS

The Postseason

After the 162-game regular season ends, four teams from the National League and four teams from the American League take part in the postseason playoffs. The teams are the winners of the three divisions (Central, East, and West) in each league, along with a wild card team from each league. The wild card team is the team with the next-best season record after the division winners.

The first round of playoff games is a best-of-five series (the first team to win three games wins). The winners then play a best-of-seven series (the first team to win four games wins) for the league championship. After this series, there are two teams left—the American League champs and the National League champs. They play each other in a best-of-seven series—the World Series.

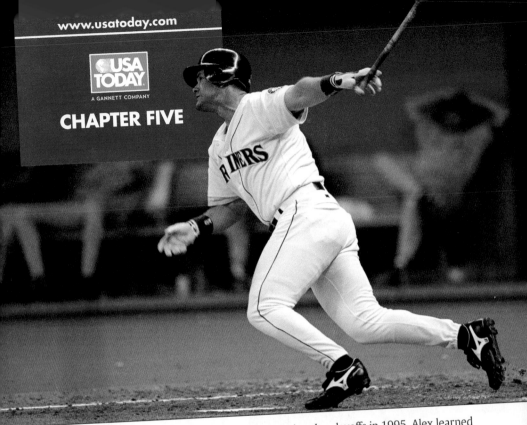

Grand slam: Edgar Martinez hits a grand slam during the playoffs in 1995. Alex learned from veterans like Martinez.

Hitting the Big Time

In the off-season, Alex went home to Miami to spend time with his family and friends. He also used his time off to study the batting patterns of a real champ. He watched tapes of Mariners teammate Edgar Martinez, who had led the American League in hitting in 1995 with a .358 average.

"The tapes were three hours long, all his hits from [1994] and [1995]," Alex later said. "I watched them about three times a week. . . . If you have a great hitter, if you have a great player, why not take the opportunities to look at them and do some of the great things they do?"

He also worked with a personal trainer to get in top physical shape. So when Alex arrived at spring training in the winter of 1996, he was ready for action. He walked up to team manager Lou Piniella and confidently said, "I'm ready." Piniella replied, "I know you are."

But Alex's first few games weren't exactly awe-inspiring. In his first 19 at bats, he got only two hits. But then, during an April 9 game in Detroit's Tiger Stadium, he hit a 440-foot home run. Within two weeks, he was hitting .375. In an April 21 game against the Toronto Blue Jays, however, Alex pulled a hamstring, a muscle in his leg. The injury put him out of commission for several weeks.

When he had healed, Alex returned to the game refreshed and charged. Piniella saw the fire in him and moved him up in the batting order from ninth to the number two spot, right in front of Ken Griffey Jr. That boost of confidence from Piniella meant a lot to Alex. He was going to run with it. Soon the one-two punch of Rodriguez and Griffey was a dangerous combination.

In the lineup: Alex bats against the Chicago White Sox during a game in June 1996.

July 9, 1996

Seattle's Rodriguez having time of young life

From the Pages of
USA TODAY

The biggest accomplishment of Alex Rodriguez's career came to him through his answering machine. He got up one morning, clicked on the machine and heard the voice of Seattle's publicity man, Dave Aust.

"He told me not only did I make the All-Star team, but I was on the cover of *Sports Illustrated*," Rodriguez said Monday as the American League worked out for tonight's All-Star Game. "I called my mom and then my high school baseball coach."

His mom, Lourdes, rushed out to buy a dozen copies of the magazine. His coach from Miami Westminster High, Rich Hofman, earned a trip to Philadelphia.

"I never dreamed of making an All-Star appearance before the age of 25," said Rodriguez, who at 20 is the 14th-youngest player to make the All-Star team.

A few comparisons: At 20, Chuck Knoblauch was in an amateur league on Cape Cod. Jeff Montgomery was in construction. Wade Boggs was in Class AA and Greg

A Star Is Born

On May 12, Alex had his first two-homer game against Kansas City. Five days later, he hit a grand slam (a homer with runners on all the bases). By June 25, he had hit 15 home runs. His batting average for June was .324. And things just kept getting better.

Alex quickly became the team heartthrob. Girls squealed when they saw him. Fans cheered his name. Attendance at home games went up by more than 10,000 per game because everyone wanted

Vaughn in Class AAA.

Rodriguez's average is .336. He has 17 home runs and 65 RBI. He plays airtight defense. He's being called Junior Jr., after teammate Ken Griffey, who broke into the big leagues at age 19.

Rodriguez wears No. 3 in honor of one of his favorite players, Dale Murphy. He used to have a Cal Ripken poster above his bed, but now he's learning firsthand from his hero. He watches Ozzie Smith highlights on videotape. He's compared to Ripken but doesn't think that is right.

"It's disrespectful to those guys," Rodriguez said. "You can mention my name with high school players, but not them."

Rodriguez likes to play computer games and ride water slides. Before he was the top pick in the '93 draft, he called the Mariners and told them he didn't want to play in Seattle and preferred the Los Angeles Dodgers.

That's because the Dodgers play in the National League and have a spring-training site in Vero Beach, Fla., close to home. The Mariners drafted him anyway. Now, he's glad to be in the Pacific Northwest.

He learns the ropes from Griffey, who knows something about breaking in at an early age. Griffey says Rodriguez handles himself well but needs work on computer games.

"He's got a long way to go to catch me, and he's not in the same league," Griffey said.

Rodriguez doesn't mind. He appreciates the side benefits of a life in the big leagues.

"Not everyone gets paid to watch Griffey play," he said.

—Mel Antonen

a glimpse of the rising superstar. And soon fans gave Alex his own nickname: A-Rod. But he didn't want to get distracted from what was most important: his game.

From June 19 to July 6, A-Rod hit in 16 of 17 games. His average rose to .341, which made him sixth in the league standings. And he wasn't even 21 years old. He was selected to play on the American League All-Star team, the youngest shortstop ever to play in an All-Star Game. Unfortunately, the National League won the game.

They're All-Stars!

In July—at the midpoint of the regular pro baseball season—Major League Baseball holds the All-Star Game. The game pits the best players from the American League against the best players from the National League. Fans vote to determine which players will take part in the game. Managers choose the pitchers.

The All-Star Game is an exhibition game. For many years, winning or losing didn't really matter. But as of 2003, the league that wins the All-Star Game gets home-field advantage during the World Series—so winning the All-Star Game has become more important.

When he returned from the All-Star matchup, A-Rod continued to heat up home plate. Teammate Ken Griffey Jr. had nothing but praise for him. "He works hard, he's a smart kid, I think he's in the right situation," Griffey told *Sports Illustrated*. "Everyone knows he's going to be a special player."

In August A-Rod's stats went through the roof. He hit .435 and was named Player of the Month, only the sixth time a Mariner had been given that honor. Then he won the American League's batting crown by having the highest average in the league. He'd hit in 52 of his last 60 games and finished the season with a .358 average. A-Rod was the third-youngest batting crown winner in AL history (after Ty Cobb and Al Kaline), and he was the first shortstop to receive the title in more than 50 years. He had 215 hits in the season, more than any other shortstop in history. On top of all of this, he had 36 homers, 3 grand slams, 123 RBIs, and a league-leading 54 doubles and 379 total bases. On the field, he was just as impressive. He'd committed just 15 errors in 657 fielding chances.

But even though the Mariners won 85 games, they finished in second place in the American League West, four games behind the Texas Rangers. They were out of the running for the postseason.

Despite that disappointment, the individual honors for A-Rod kept streaming in. The Associated Press and *Sporting News* named him Player of the Year. He didn't win the league's Most Valuable Player award (two baseball writers from each team's city vote on the MVP), but he was just three votes behind the Texas Rangers' Juan Gonzalez for the honor.

High praise came from his childhood idol, Cal Ripken Jr. "All that Alex seems to need is experience to become the shortstop everyone else will be watching in our league," Ripken said. "The future belongs to Alex Rodriguez."

USA TODAY Snapshots®

One-team players

Most games by players who played entire career with one franchise:

Carl Yastrzemski	Red Sox	3,308
Stan Musial	Cardinals	3,026
Cal Ripken Jr.	Orioles	3,001
Brooks Robinson	Orioles	2,896
Robin Yount	Brewers	2,856
Craig Biggio	Astros	2,850

Source: USA TODAY research

By Matt Young and Frank Pompa, USA TODAY, 2010

"Alex's composure and maturity level are impressive. A lot of players come in with raw talent, but they don't know how to play or handle themselves off the field. Alex does both well."

—Cal Ripken Jr.

Giving Back

A-Rod played another role off the field. As a Latino—a person of Latin American heritage—he was a role model for young Latino boys and girls. A-Rod took this job very seriously. "I'm proud to be an American and proud that my parents are Dominican," he said.

A-Rod used his new-found fame to do positive things. He was always willing to meet and greet fans and sign autographs. He visited Seattle-area grade schools and encouraged students to focus on reading, math, physical fitness, and good citizenship. He'd say things like, "Math is very important, to keep up with Ken Griffey's batting average." Learning had always been important to A-Rod, and he wanted to instill that love in his young fans.

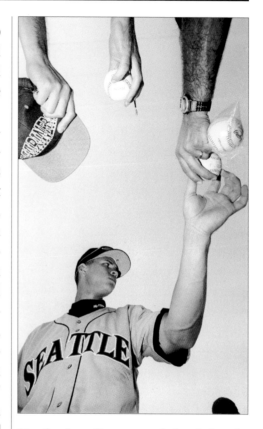

Meeting fans: Alex autographs baseballs and hats for fans after a Mariners' game in 1996.

When A-Rod returned home to Florida after the season, he went back to the place that had nurtured his love for baseball—the Hank Kline Club. He visited his pal and former coach Eddy Rodriguez and gave him some happy news: A-Rod was donating $25,000 to build a new baseball field behind the club. "No other player has ever come back to this place and given like Alex has," Rodriguez said. "Alex just did it. 'Whatever you need,' he said."

A-Rod also bought a new house for himself, just a few blocks from his mother's home in Kendall. He played golf with pal Derek Jeter, who had become a close friend since they first spoke during the younger player's senior year of high school. He also decided to buy a home in Seattle, since he was settled in with the Mariners.

 "Although being a millionaire at age eighteen changed my material value, it hasn't changed my personal values. It's not how much you make that counts. It's what you do with it."

—Alex Rodriguez

Then an offer came along that A-Rod couldn't resist. He was asked to go to Japan with a team of star major leaguers to play a series of exhibition games (games played just for show). Cal Ripken Jr. was a member of the team. During their time in Japan, A-Rod got to know his hero. "We spent time together every day. I learned so much, not just about baseball, but about life," A-Rod said. "What I learned from Cal is to respect the game, respect the fans. Nothing fancy out there. Just do your job."

At the start of the 1997 season, that's exactly what 21-year-old A-Rod did. By mid-April he was batting .333. During a hot hitting streak beginning in June, A-Rod achieved a memorable feat. In a June 5

IN FOCUS

Wall of Honor

A-Rod was such a fan of Baltimore Orioles star shortstop Cal Ripken Jr. that when A-Rod moved into his own home, he took an old poster of Ripken from his childhood days, framed it, and put it up in the new house.

Hitting for the cycle: Alex returns to the dugout after scoring a run in the fourth inning of the Mariners' June 5, 1997, game against the Detroit Tigers.

game against the Detroit Tigers, he hit for the cycle, which means he hit a single, a double, a triple, and a home run in the same game. He was only the second Mariner ever to accomplish this feat (Jay Buhner had been the first).

Team Effort

A-Rod's teammates were also doing well. Pitcher Randy Johnson, who had been injured during the 1996 season, was helping lead the team to victory. Edgar Martinez, whose batting style A-Rod had once studied, was one of the league's leading hitters. And Ken Griffey Jr. had hit 30 home runs by the All-Star break (midway through the season). Meanwhile, once again A-Rod was picked to be the starting shortstop at the All-Star Game.

After the All-Star break, A-Rod and his teammates were playing spectacularly. They won the American League West title and then faced the Baltimore Orioles—Cal Ripken's team—in the playoffs. Unfortunately, they lost in the first round to the Orioles, three games to one. That was the end of the Mariners' postseason.

When the 1997 season wrapped up, A-Rod wanted to stay out of the limelight as much as he could. He worked on writing a children's book, *Alex Rodriguez: Hit a Grand Slam!*, with the help of sportswriter Greg Brown. And in January, he took a college class. "My continuing education is so important to me that I took my first college courses," he wrote. "I'm determined to get a college degree someday. I don't care if it takes me ten years."

A-Rod also went back to the Hank Kline Club to work out with coach Eddy Rodriguez. There A-Rod received a special honor. A new baseball field for which he'd donated money was named the Alex Rodriguez Baseball Field. "I'm really proud of that," A-Rod said. "It's got a bronze statue of me out in front and my picture on a wall."

All stars: Alex *(left)* and teammate Ken Griffey Jr. talk while participating in pre-All-Star Game activities in 1997.

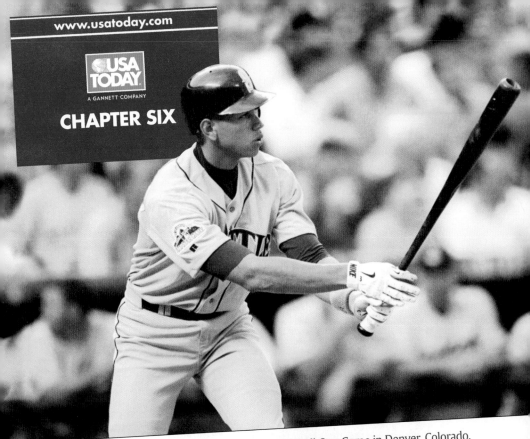

Big bat: Alex focuses on the pitcher during the 1998 All-Star Game in Denver, Colorado.

Seeing 40-40

A-Rod continued his work with young people during the winter of 1997. He put on baseball clinics to teach elementary-school-age baseball players the basics of the game. He also wanted to nurture a young person on a more personal level. Before the start of the 1998 season, he decided to help out an underprivileged Miami boy and show him a better way of life. A-Rod took him to charity functions and even let the boy stay at his house when he wasn't there.

"Speaking at schools has shown me that sometimes encouragement is the best gift, and that doesn't cost anything."

—Alex Rodriguez

But one day, after A-Rod returned from a trip, he found his home vandalized, his expensive suits stolen, and more than $100,000 in cash missing. Even his All-Star Game jersey, with Cal Ripken's signature on it, was gone. The thief was the young man A-Rod had tried to help. "I felt violated.... There is no other way to describe it," A-Rod told reporters. He had trusted someone who had taken terrible advantage of him. From then on, Alex was going to be a lot more careful about how and whom he helped. It was a valuable lesson for the trusting young player.

In June Alex batted .328 for the month and was chosen as the American League's starting shortstop for the All-Star Game, where he knocked out a homer and helped the AL win 13–8. Home runs were becoming the norm for A-Rod. In mid-July, he slammed balls out of the park in three straight games, and on July 19, he hit his 30th round-tripper of the season. Two weeks later, he stole his 29th and 30th bases of the year in a game against the Yankees. There to congratulate him on joining the 30-30 Club (30 home runs and 30 stolen bases in a season) was pal Derek Jeter, the Yanks' shortstop.

While he was having an astounding season, some of his Mariners teammates weren't having a great time. Star pitcher Randy Johnson, the anchor of the Mariners pitching staff, asked to be traded because he wasn't happy with the team's overall record. He was sent to the Houston Astros. In his place, a crop of young pitchers came on board.

The team as a whole wasn't performing exceptionally. By the end of August, the Mariners were in last place in the AL West with a 61–71 record.

But A-Rod wasn't going to give up on the rest of the season. On September 8, he hit his 39th home run of the year, and two days later, he stole his 41st base. Then on September 19, he hit a home run in the first inning against Anaheim Angels pitcher Jack McDowell. He was now an official member—the third ever—of the 40-40 Club (40 homers and 40 stolen bases).

Three days later, A-Rod hit his 41st homer against the Oakland Athletics, breaking the American League record for homers by a shortstop (Rico Petrocelli had hit 40 in 1969). By season's end, A-Rod had hit his 42nd.

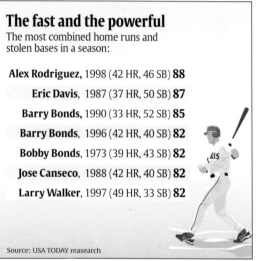

USA TODAY Snapshots®

The fast and the powerful

The most combined home runs and stolen bases in a season:

Alex Rodriguez, 1998 (42 HR, 46 SB) **88**

Eric Davis, 1987 (37 HR, 50 SB) **87**

Barry Bonds, 1990 (33 HR, 52 SB) **85**

Barry Bonds, 1996 (42 HR, 40 SB) **82**

Bobby Bonds, 1973 (39 HR, 43 SB) **82**

Jose Canseco, 1988 (42 HR, 40 SB) **82**

Larry Walker, 1997 (49 HR, 33 SB) **82**

Source: USA TODAY reasearch

By Ellen J. Horrow and Adrienne Lewis, USA TODAY, 2001

IN FOCUS

Join the Club

In 1988 Jose Canseco, a right fielder with the Oakland Athletics, became the first ballplayer to hit 40 home runs and steal 40 bases in a single season. He was 24 years old. Barry Bonds of the San Francisco Giants became the second member of that club in 1996 at the age of 32. A-Rod was just 23 years old when he joined the club in 1998. Coincidentally, all three ballplayers celebrate birthdays in the month of July.

September 25, 1998

Remarkable '98 season is one for the (history) books

From the Pages of
<u>USA TODAY</u>

Of all the eye-popping achievements that have been sprinkled throughout the 1998 baseball season there is one that stands alone, one that not long ago was unthinkable:

For the first time in years, baseball can keep a perfectly straight face while referring to itself as the national pastime.

Throughout the 1998 season there have been monster achievements that in many other recent seasons would have provided the year's highlight.

Evidence that baseball is enjoying renewed popularity this season came in a USA TODAY/CNN/Gallup Poll in mid-September in which 63% of the respondents identified themselves as a fan or somewhat of a fan. In June, only 44% said that. Baseball also has a chance to set an all-time attendance record if it averages 26,566 fans at the remaining games.

If there is a downside to the 1998 season, perhaps it is that such accomplishments have been eclipsed by Mark McGwire and Sammy Sosa breaking Roger Maris' single-season record of 61 home runs. Among the other performances that have been overshadowed:

Seattle's Ken Griffey Jr. also surpassing the 50-homer mark, giving baseball three hitters with that many home runs in a single season for the first time. San Diego's Greg Vaughn, with 49 homers going into the weekend, could make it four.

San Francisco's Barry Bonds, becoming the first player ever to have 400 home runs and 400 stolen bases in a career.

Seattle shortstop Alex Rodriguez making the prestigious 40-40 tandem for home runs and stolen bases. He hit his 42nd homer Wednesday night and has 44 stolen bases. In 1988, that was the credential that virtually won the American League Most Valuable Player award for Jose Canseco. In 1998, Rodriguez will be fortunate to finish in the top 10 for MVP voting.

—Tom Weir

Overcoming Injury

During the 1998 season, A-Rod played in every game, batted .310, and led the league with 213 hits, 686 at bats, and 64 multi-hit games. He also stole 46 bases and made only 18 errors on the field. The Mariners ultimately ended up in third place in the AL West with a 76–85 record.

"I want to be known as a good major leaguer, and good major leaguers work to become good."

—Alex Rodriguez

With the season ending, A-Rod returned to his charity work. He created the Alex Rodriguez Foundation, a children's charity. And along with military and political leader Colin Powell and actor Denzel Washington, he became a spokesperson for the Boys & Girls Clubs of America. Around this time, A-Rod also began dating Cynthia Scurtis, a

Dating: Alex and Cynthia Scurtis attend a Miami Heat basketball game in Miami in 2001.

Miami high school psychology teacher. Things were coming into place in his life.

The ballplayer felt clearheaded and ready for the 1999 season. But two games in, A-Rod twisted his left knee and tore some cartilage. He had to undergo surgery, and he missed 32 games.

During this time, many people questioned whether the star short-stop would stick with the Mariners. A-Rod was honest about the fact that he wanted to go to the World Series. On a website devoted to A-Rod, he wrote about talking with Mariners management about putting together a championship team with solid players.

With A-Rod sidelined, the Mariners fell into a slump. They were 15–20 before he returned to the fold in a May 21 game against the Kansas City Royals. With his knee healed, A-Rod was back in fine form, and at his first at bat, he homered. Then he helped lead his team to a six-game winning streak, during which he hit .304 with three homers.

After losing the next two games, the Mariners bounced back and were victorious in four games. Their record jumped back over .500 (more wins than losses) to 25–24.

A-Rod then went on a 13-game hitting streak, raising his average to .357. And during a game against the Orioles, he stole the 100th base of his career. But in August, after hitting his 34th and 35th home runs of the year in a game against the Chicago White Sox, he went into a slump. He batted .104 over the next month, and his season average fell to .287. He turned things around on September 16 when he hit a grand slam in the eighth inning against Tampa Bay Rays (formerly known as the Devil Rays).

A Complete Player

Unfortunately, once again the Mariners weren't going to the postseason. For the second year in a row, they finished third in the American League West, this time with a 79–83 record. One of the bright spots of the season was that the team had a new home stadium, the open-air Safeco Field, which replaced the smaller, enclosed Kingdome.

Go the Distance

In 1999 Seattle Mariners fans were thrilled when the old Kingdome was replaced by the new Safeco Field. But the new stadium gave A-Rod and his teammates a challenge. Since the new stadium was much bigger than the old dome, it was more difficult to hit home runs there.

A new diamond: The Mariners play their first game at Safeco Field on July 15, 1999.

Ultimately A-Rod ended the 1999 season with a .285 average. But he had driven in 111 runs, knocked in 42 homers, stolen 21 bases, and hit 25 doubles. Despite his overall good season, much of the attention that year was focused on the home run race between Mark McGwire, Sammy Sosa, and A-Rod's teammate Ken Griffey Jr.

Even though Alex wasn't the center of attention, people were still taking notice of him. "He's a complete player," said Rudy Terrasas, a scout for the Texas Rangers. "He can beat you in all facets of the game—with his power, his speed, and his glove. And he's still young, with a tremendous upside. People who play like he does are usually twenty-eight, twenty-nine, thirty years old. He's not even twenty-four and doing it. For my money, if I was starting a club and needed a shortstop . . . he'd be my choice." With the 2000 season ahead of him, A-Rod was going to have some interesting choices to make.

IN FOCUS

Mark McGwire

Mark McGwire made quite an impression in 1987, his rookie year. Playing for the Oakland Athletics, he set a record for most home runs by a rookie, with 49. The six foot five first baseman was known as a power hitter throughout his career. In 1997 McGwire was traded to the St. Louis Cardinals mid-season. The following year he slammed 70 home runs, setting a new record for home runs in a single season. The previous record holder was Roger Maris, a member of the New York Yankees who hit 61 homers in 1961.

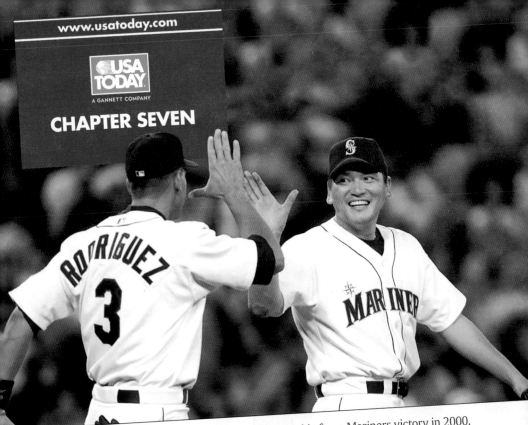

High five: Alex congratulates pitcher Kazuhiro Sasaki after a Mariners victory in 2000. Sasaki was one of the new faces brought to the Mariners for the 2000 season.

New Faces, New Places

■■■■

With the close of the 1999 season, questions were flying about whether A-Rod would re-sign with the Mariners. His contract was going to expire after the 2000 season, and he would be a free agent, able to choose whatever team he'd like to play for next.

In October 1999, Mariners chairman Howard Lincoln told the media that he'd make offers to both A-Rod and Ken Griffey Jr. that would make them the highest-paid players in baseball. Griffey told A-Rod to keep his mind on his game, not on the contract negotiations. But A-Rod couldn't help but think about them. "I've never been under such a microscope," he said in an interview with the *Sporting News*. "I'm not experienced with this. It's not like fielding a ground ball or hitting the curve."

Before the 2000 season began, Griffey decided it was time to make a move. He requested a trade to the Cincinnati Reds. The trade was a big deal for A-Rod, who'd always looked up to Griffey, the first person he became friends with when he joined the Mariners. There had been some rivalry between the two star players over the years, yet they also had a special connection. "It's like a big brother-little brother relationship," explained Griffey.

To many people's surprise, the Mariners had a strong 2000 season. With powerhouse pitchers Aaron Sele and Kazuhiro Sasaki and first baseman John Olerud on board, they had shored up their lineup. As they moved toward the postseason, it was clear that this time, they had a shot at going to the playoffs. "We're having a blast," said A-Rod.

IN F CUS

Ken Griffey Jr.

Ken Griffey Jr. grew up in Cincinnati, Ohio, where he learned to play baseball from a major leaguer—his father, Ken Griffey Sr. Griffey Sr. played outfield for the Cincinnati Reds from 1973 to 1981. The Seattle Mariners drafted Griffey Jr. in 1987, and in 1990 and 1991, father and son played together for the Mariners. Griffey Jr. is known for his great home-run production and his outstanding abilities in center field.

Back to the Playoffs

As the last day of the season approached, the Mariners played the Oakland Athletics (also known as the Oakland A's) for the division title. And even though the A's beat Seattle, the Mariners weren't out of the running for the postseason. Because they had the best record of the teams that didn't win their divisions, the Mariners qualified for the postseason wild card spot.

In the first round of the playoffs—the American League Division Series—Seattle faced the Chicago White Sox. The Mariners knew it would be key to have strong pitching and keep White Sox slugger Frank Thomas from scoring. Game one took place in Chicago's U.S. Cellular Field. For nine innings, the game was close. The teams were tied 4–4 at the end of the ninth. In the top of the 10th, Edgar Martinez hit a two-run home run and John Olerud followed that up with a solo homer. Chicago didn't manage to score at all in the bottom of the inning, giving the Mariners a 7–4 victory.

The Mariners needed only nine innings to win game two 5–2. Then they headed back to Safeco Field, where they planned to finish off the series in front of a hometown crowd. Game three was close, but Seattle pulled off a 2–1 win. They were one step closer to the World Series!

The Mariners were up against the New York Yankees in their quest for the American League pennant, or championship. The team that won the American League Championship Series would go to the World Series. On paper, the Mariners looked good. They had a 91–71 regular season record, compared with New York's 87–74 record. But New York had a lot of playoff experience and had won the World Series in 1998 and 1999.

In the first matchup, Mariners pitcher Freddy Garcia's fiery arm kept the Yanks from scoring any runs. The Mariners took a 1–0 lead into the sixth inning. Then A-Rod came to bat with no one on base against Yankees pitcher Denny Neagle. He hit a foul ball on a 3–1 count (three balls, one strike), making the count 3–2. On the next pitch, Neagle threw A-Rod a fastball. That was just what Alex needed. He powered a home run to left field. Seattle took a 2–0 lead and won the game.

There was electricity in the air. Could the Mariners beat the Yanks again?

In game two, the Mariners took an early lead, but the Yankees seemed determined to crush the Mariners' World Series hopes. A-Rod's pal Derek Jeter hit a two-run homer in the eighth inning to help his team to a 7–1 victory.

The series moved to Seattle for the next three games. But the Yankees continued to dominate, winning game three 8–2 and game four 5–0. One more win would give the Yankees the pennant. The Mariners played hard in game five, and they pulled off a 6–2 win. Alex batted in two runs in the fifth inning to contribute to the win.

Game six took place back at Yankee Stadium. Even after New York was leading 9–4 in the seventh inning, Seattle didn't give up. A-Rod started off the eighth inning with a home run, and the Mariners followed up with two more runs, but that was all they could manage. The final score was New York 9, Seattle 7. The Mariners' promising season had come to a disappointing end.

Strike out: Alex shows his frustration after striking out in the third inning of game six of the ALCS in 2000.

Uncertain Future

Overall, A-Rod had had a great season in 2000, hitting .316 and 41 homers, scoring a career-best 132 RBIs, earning 34 doubles and 134 runs, drawing 100 walks, and committing only 10 errors. In the ALCS, he had a stellar .409 batting average. When asked if he planned on staying with the Mariners for another season, A-Rod answered carefully. "I absolutely see scenarios where I'm in Seattle next year," he said. "But at the same time, I see scenarios where I'm elsewhere."

"If they go out and get the pieces [championship-level players], sure, I'd be more than willing to sign with the Mariners."

—Alex Rodriguez, on whether he would re-sign with Seattle

A-Rod was a huge prospect for other teams. By then he was on the free-agent market, and ball clubs were vying for him. Everybody wanted a piece of Alex Rodriguez. Wherever he went in Seattle, whether it was his favorite restaurant or the clubhouse, scouts would follow. He was on everyone's hit list.

Many thought that if he left the

USA TODAY Snapshots®

You ought to be in pictures

Sports celebrities that people[1] would most like to be photographed with:

Muhammad Ali — 24%
Shaquille O'Neal — 23%
Tiger Woods — 23%
Alex Rodriguez — 13%
Wayne Gretzky — 9%
Tom Brady — 8%

1 – More than 37,000 respondents were surveyed
Source: *Popular Photography & Imaging* and America Online

By Ellen J. Horrow and Alejandro Gonzalez, USA TODAY, 2004

Mariners, he would go to the New York Mets or the Los Angeles Dodgers, the team he had wanted to join when he was in high school. But these teams didn't pursue him. A-Rod's agent, Scott Boras, was asking for a $200 million contract. For some teams, A-Rod was too expensive. The Atlanta Braves and the New York Yankees passed on him, and eventually the Mariners decided not to bid for him anymore. But many other teams were still chasing him. It became a favorite game among sportswriters to guess which team A-Rod would sign with.

In December, A-Rod would have to make a decision. Everybody's eyes were on him. What would he do? By then the Chicago White Sox and the Texas Rangers were the only two teams willing to pay the $200 million asking price.

Getting Paid

After weeks of negotiations, on December 11, 2000, A-Rod signed an astonishing $252 million contract, to be paid out over 10 years, with the Texas Rangers (based near Dallas in Arlington, Texas). The contract made A-Rod the highest-paid athlete in the history of professional sports.

A new team: Alex announces his move to the Texas Rangers at a press conference in December 2000. Behind him are his agent, Scott Boras *(left)*, and Rangers owner Tom Hicks *(right)*.

Rodriguez has mixed feelings

From the Pages of
USA TODAY

After six weeks of deciding where to play baseball in 2001, shortstop Alex Rodriguez, newest member of the Texas Rangers, is happy the process is over. He said it was crazy and thought it would never end.

And, now comes the hard part: Calling Edgar Martinez, his former teammate with the Seattle Mariners, and explaining his decision to sign a $252 million, 10-year contract with the rival Rangers. Martinez, who had to deal with the shock of losing Ken Griffey Jr., had been calling Rodriguez every day, saying to stay in Seattle.

"It's going to be a tough call," Rodriguez said after his first Rangers news conference at The Ballpark in Arlington on Tuesday afternoon. "Edgar kept saying he was going to retire if I didn't come back. I don't want that responsibility."

Rodriguez knows he will be criticized for the contract and that it will be a lightning rod for all the problems in the industry. He's heard the critics say team owner Tom Hicks was a fool for handing out that much money.

The same was said when Pedro Martinez, Kevin Brown and Greg Maddux switched teams, Rodriguez said: "Only time will tell, and (I hope) champions are fools."

His agent, Scott Boras, called the criticism unfair, especially that of Major League Baseball vice president Sandy Alderson, former general manager with Oakland.

Boras said Alderson is critical of the same system that he used to be competitive, when he had players that had some of the highest salaries in the game.

"And the Oakland franchise is still around," Boras said.

How he's going to spend the money? Rodriguez doesn't know. "I'm going to do good things for good people," he answered.

He doesn't mind moving from a rainy, cold climate to the heat of Texas. Rodriguez reminded everyone that he grew up in Miami.

"That's going to be a positive adjustment," Rodriguez said. "I enjoy the heat."

Rodriguez said he was in Las Vegas playing golf when Boras closed the deal Sunday, about 11 P.M. CT. He had mixed emotions.

"You are leaving Seattle and a lot of long friendships," he said. "I was excited, but disappointed. What was making me happy was also making me sad."

—Mel Antonen

A-Rod's contract included a no-trade clause (which meant he couldn't be traded without his approval) plus an escape clause that granted him the right to become a free agent after seven years. The Rangers also agreed to up his pay if another player signed for more money than he made. For example, if another player signed a contract for $300 million, A-Rod's salary would go up to $301 million, and he would remain the highest-paid player in baseball.

"If there's a player deserving of the largest contract in baseball, it's this player."

—Tom Hicks, owner of the Texas Rangers from 1998 to 2010

A-Rod had always said he wanted to play for a winning team, so it came as a surprise to some people that he signed with the Rangers. The Rangers lost 91 games in 2000 and had won only one postseason contest since the team had formed in 1972. Yet A-Rod saw an opportunity to make the Rangers a victorious squad. He also wanted to work hard and prove that he was worth the big money he was earning.

It was an exciting but crazy time for A-Rod. Everyone wanted to talk to—and write about—this $252 million man. Everyone from gum manufacturers to vacuum cleaner and car companies wanted to pay him to be a spokesperson. A slew of endorsement offers came his way.

It was time for him to get some peace. He sold his home in Seattle and returned home to Miami, where he could spend time with his mom, his girlfriend, and his friends. He would need all the support he could get. A-Rod had a big year—and a lot of changes—ahead of him.

New team, new fans: Alex signs autographs for fans during the 2001 season.

Most Valuable Player

A-Rod enjoyed his time home in Miami over the holiday season. He hung out with Cynthia and his dog Ripper (named after his hero Cal Ripken) and relaxed by playing golf and boating on the Atlantic Ocean.

On Christmas morning 2000, A-Rod's mom, Lourdes, gave him a meaningful present: a book about Leonardo da Vinci, whom A-Rod had admired since he was a little boy. Also during the holidays, A-Rod and his entire family went to the Dominican Republic. When they returned home, A-Rod had a party with his friends and family to celebrate his buying a new boat, appropriately named *Sweet Swing*. He docked the boat near his home in Miami.

 A-Rod loves hip-hop music (Jay-Z is one of his favorite artists), singer Mariah Carey, and the legendary rock group the Rolling Stones.

But soon it was time to get back to work. Since he was the highest-paid athlete in professional sports, A-Rod knew that expectations for him were sky-high. Former teammate Ken Griffey Jr. cautioned him that he was in for his "most challenging year."

Along with A-Rod, other major batters on the Rangers team included All-Star catcher Ivan "Pudge" Rodriguez, who'd hit .347 in 2000, and first baseman Rafael Palmeiro, a powerhouse home-run hitter. Where the Rangers were weak was in their pitching. But despite Hicks's efforts, no star pitchers were interested in joining the Rangers. Without a strong pitching staff, it would be hard to be real competitors.

Still, when A-Rod showed up for spring training in Port Charlotte, Florida, he was determined to make 2001 a great season. He could barely believe the crowds who came out to see him. People swarmed him for photos and autographs. As always, A-Rod was polite and chatted with fans. Like his idol Cal Ripken, he knew the importance of being a good person and not just a great player. He didn't take any of the attention for granted.

Back to Seattle

When the 2001 season started, A-Rod was fired up and ready to go. The Rangers opened the season by traveling to San Juan, Puerto Rico, to play the Toronto Blue Jays. (Major League Baseball likes to send its teams to different parts of the world to expose new fans to the game.) A-Rod was nervous but excited.

In the first inning, he got a base hit. But things got worse from there. First, he fielded a grounder but wildly threw the ball past first base. Then, when trying to execute a double play, the 25-year-old tripped on his own shoelaces and fell. The Rangers lost 8–1. "You have to start somewhere," A-Rod said after the game. "[The game] had a little of everything—error, slip, hit. . . . You just move on."

Keeping focus: Alex gets ready to bat while being booed by Mariners fans during his first game back in Seattle after signing with the Rangers.

In mid-April, A-Rod and the Rangers headed to Seattle to play their first game against the Mariners. A-Rod didn't exactly get the welcome of an old friend. Instead, he faced boos and hisses from fans who felt he'd betrayed the Mariners by leaving them. But A-Rod wasn't angry about the cold reception. He understood the Mariners fans' disappointment.

By May the Rangers slipped in the standings and had lost 14 out of 25 games. The front office decided it was time to shake things up and replaced manager Johnny Oates with Jerry Narron. That change gave the guys on the team a morale boost. Then A-Rod helped things when he got his 1,000th career hit off pitcher Gary Glover of the Chicago White Sox.

In July A-Rod was once again part of the All-Star Game. This time he switched positions so that his idol Cal Ripken could play shortstop in his final All-Star Game before retiring. A-Rod happily took third base. Even though the game was played in Seattle, that generous gesture gave A-Rod a round of cheers from the fans in the stands.

Star turn: Alex goofs off with Cal Ripken during the 2001 All-Star Game. Alex played third base so that Ripken could play shortstop.

In 2001 A-Rod was named one of *People* magazine's "50 Most Beautiful People in the World."

In September A-Rod hit his 48th home run of the season off Anaheim Angel Ramon Ortiz. With that achievement, he bypassed Chicago Cubs legend Ernie Banks for the most homers in a season by a shortstop. Banks sent Alex a message: "Congratulations to A-Rod. I knew you could do it. You are a great man, an impressive baseball player, and a role model. I love the game of baseball, and I love to see players with heart and drive like yours who continue the spirit of the game."

Personal Success

Despite A-Rod's winning play, the Rangers had a less-than-impressive season. They ended with a record of 73 wins and 89 losses and landed in last place in the American League West.

But A-Rod had lived up to management's expectations. He had hit .318, played in all 162 games, led the American League in home runs (he had hit 52 by season's end), and had 135 RBIs and 201 hits. He also became the fourth player ever (and the first since Detroit Tiger Jimmie Foxx in 1932) to hit more than 50 home runs and collect 200 hits in a single season. Although A-Rod didn't get picked as the American League's MVP (the Seattle Mariners' new outfielder Ichiro Suzuki won, and A-Rod finished in sixth place in the voting), he was honored with the Hank Aaron Award as the AL's best hitter.

"Alex has played tremendously well," said teammate Gabe Kapler. "We've gotten everything we could have possibly hoped for from Alex Rodriguez." And one major-league scout raved, "His team scuffled but he still dived for balls even when his team was down 10–1. He plays hard all the time. He plays the game right."

Meanwhile, the Mariners had a great season. They won 116 games and made the playoffs. It was a bittersweet time for A-Rod.

At the end of April 2002, A-Rod hit his 250th home run. The 26-year-old became the second-youngest player (behind Jimmie Foxx) to reach that mark. He was playing well, and in June, he was elected to the All-Star team for the fifth year in a row. On his 27th birthday, on July 27, he hit a grand slam, his 34th homer of the season. And in a series against Toronto in September, A-Rod hit six homers in three games. He was only the fourth player in the history of Major League Baseball to reach that milestone.

"He's the best player I've seen."

—Carlos Tosca, former Toronto Blue Jays manager, about A-Rod

But his team wasn't following suit. The Rangers finished the season with a 72–90 record. They were last in the American League West for the second season in a row.

Although his team had crumbled, A-Rod had shone during the season. He led both leagues with 57 home runs (the second-highest total for a right-handed hitter in American League history), 142 RBIs, and 389 total bases and became the first player to lead the majors in all three categories since Tony Armas of the Boston Red Sox had done it in 1984. He had also hit .300 and driven in 142 runs.

MVP?

In the past, A-Rod had never publicly expressed his desire to be voted the league's Most Valuable Player. But this time, he was verbal about his hopes. "Sure, I'd be disappointed if I'm not the MVP," he said. "I've been in the race a few times. I've come close. I deserve it."

But Oakland A's shortstop Miguel Tejada was chosen MVP, and A-Rod came in second place. Tejada came in ahead of A-Rod, many thought, because the A's had made the playoffs and the Rangers hadn't even been in contention.

A-Rod had to put that loss behind him. He had other things to focus on. He continued working on his charitable efforts. In October he made a $3.9 million contribution to the baseball program at the University of Miami, the school he'd almost attended. Most of the money went toward renovating the baseball stadium he used to sneak

September 18, 2002

Top shortstops long on talent

From the Pages of
<u>USA TODAY</u>

USA TODAY's Mel Antonen and Cesar Brioso break down the Fab Four of baseball's glamour position: Alex Rodriguez, Miguel Tejada, Nomar Garciaparra and Derek Jeter, who keep adding pop to a position formerly all about defense. They continue what Cal Ripken began, revolutionizing play at shortstop.

The A-Rod File

Name: Alex Rodriguez.

Team: Texas Rangers.

Age: 27.

2002 Salary: $22 million.

Key stat: A-Rod, who leads the American League in home runs and RBI, is the fifth player to record successive 50-homer seasons, joining Babe Ruth, Mark McGwire, Sammy Sosa and Ken Griffey Jr.

Background: Born in New York, Rodriguez and family moved to Miami. Rodriguez's father walked out on the family while Alex was in grade school. He grew up idolizing Cal Ripken.

into as a child. "This is my Yankee Stadium, my Candlestick Park, my Dodger Stadium," A-Rod said at the opening ceremony for the new stadium. "I used to jump the fence. They had high trees over there. I fell a few times, but I still got in. I remember being sad on Sundays when the sun went down because I had to wait another week to see the [University of Miami] Hurricanes play." A-Rod also revealed to the press that he wanted to return to the school one day to get his bachelor's degree in literature.

Appeal: Professionalism. He hasn't let the pressure of having the richest contract in sports history or the frustration of playing on terrible teams keep him from showing he might be the best player in baseball.

Worst thing to say about him: His 10-year, $252 million contract makes it difficult for the Rangers to surround him with enough talented players to win. Texas is on its way toward finishing last in the AL West for the second season in a row with A-Rod in the fold.

Endorsements: Teamed with Daisy Fuentes to promote RadioShack. Also endorses Colgate, Mennen Speed Stick, Nike.

Dating: Engaged to longtime girlfriend Cynthia Scurtis, a high school psychology teacher; their wedding is scheduled for November.

Items on eBay: 2,518.

Favorite movie: *Major League.*

Reading: *Jack: Straight From the Gut*, former General Electric CEO Jack Welch's autobiography.

In the offseason: Spends time in Dallas, where he owns a home and has season tickets to the Mavericks.

Scouting report

He's the sport's best all-around player and has the best chance to win a Triple Crown, especially in the Rangers' roomy home ballpark. . . . Throws three-quarters and might have the strongest arm among shortstops, given his ability to throw from deep in the hole. . . . Biggest improvement is more accurate throws to first from behind second base. . . . Needs to work on catching routine popups. . . . Wants to increase his average to the .340 range and on-base percentage to .440. He could push 75 homers in a season. He will become extra dangerous when he stops swinging at bad pitches trying for the long ball.

—Mel Antonen and Cesar Brioso

A-Rod had another big moment on November 2, 2002. He married his longtime sweetheart Cynthia Scurtis in a private wedding ceremony, held at a home A-Rod had purchased in the Highland Park section of Dallas. Cal Ripken was one of the guests.

Later that month, A-Rod got a boost in his career when he was honored with his first-ever Gold Glove Award, thanks to his supreme performance on the field: only 10 errors in 741 chances. The Gold Glove is awarded to the league's best fielder at each position.

MVP

In February 2003, A-Rod headed for spring training in Surprise, Arizona. Changes were afoot. Manager Jerry Narron had been replaced with former Yankee and Arizona Diamondbacks manager Buck Showalter. Pitchers Ugueth Urbina and Esteban Yan were also brought on board.

But on his first day of playing in training, A-Rod felt a stabbing pain above his shoulders. He went to the doctor and was diagnosed with a herniated (ruptured) disk in his neck. Luckily, he was healed by the time the season opened against the Anaheim Angels on April 2, 2003. In this game, he hit his 300th career home run off pitcher Ramon Ortiz, becoming the youngest player (27 years, 249 days) to achieve that honor.

Once again, though, the Rangers were in trouble. By the end of May, they were heading to last place. Owner Tom Hicks even began trading away some of the team's higher-priced players to give some rookies a chance.

By the end of July, after A-Rod was again selected to play in the All-Star Game, the Rangers were losing regularly. At a press conference, A-Rod said he wanted to be part of a winning team that could make it to the World Series.

A-Rod's words seemed to spark his teammates. By August the team had an improved record of 57 wins and 57 losses. But that improvement was short-lived. By September the

New record: Alex hits career home run number 300, becoming the youngest player to do so at the age of 27.

Rangers were in a slump, and A-Rod did something he'd never done: he broke his streak of playing 546 games in a row and sat out a game in frustration.

By season's end, the Rangers had a 71–91 record, finishing in last place in the American League West and 25 games behind the division-winning Oakland A's. The Rangers' pitching hadn't been strong enough, and the lineup hadn't been powerful.

USA TODAY Snapshots®

Baseball's RBI men

Ken Griffey Jr. ranks 16th and Manny Ramirez 19th on the all-time RBI list.
Active leaders in RBI:

Player	RBI
Ken Griffey Jr.	1,829
Manny Ramirez	1,788
Alex Rodriguez	1,706
Gary Sheffield	1,676
Jim Thome	1,565

Source: MLB.com

By Matt Eppers and Web Bryant, USA TODAY, 2009

A-Rod had definitely done his part for the team. He had hit .298, won the American League home run title for the third year in a row with 47 home runs, finished the season with a league-high 124 runs, and made only 8 errors in 158 games. But A-Rod's great season personally didn't change the fact that he was playing for a losing team.

His contributions would be recognized, though. In November he was given the Gold Glove, the Silver Slugger Award, and the Hank Aaron Award. On November 18, 2003, he was named the Most Valuable Player in the American League, beating out Carlos Delgado of the Toronto Blue Jays. It was a huge achievement, one he had been wanting for a long time.

Alex had a lot on his mind. When he spoke to reporters after winning the MVP honors, he said he felt "humbled and overwhelmed." But he also admitted that he would approve a trade if it allowed him to go to a winning team. He had to decide whether to stay with Texas or go elsewhere.

Back to New York: Alex announces his trade to the New York Yankees on February 17, 2004, moving him back to the city where he was born.

Blue-and-White Stripes

The New York Yankees were interested in A-Rod. They already had a top shortstop, Derek Jeter. But their third baseman, Aaron Boone, had badly injured his ankle in a game of pick-up basketball and would have to sit out the entire season. The Yankees wanted A-Rod on board as their new third baseman, if he would agree to switch positions.

In early February, A-Rod returned to Texas as the new Rangers team captain. Although he admitted his frustration, A-Rod told reporters that following a five-hour discussion with team owner Tom Hicks and manager Buck Showalter, he felt the team had some hope for the 2004 season.

"After that meeting, I felt like the Rangers had a great plan in hand," said A-Rod. "I felt very comfortable about where the Texas Rangers were heading. As long as the train was moving forward and in the right direction, that was all I wanted to see."

Although it appeared A-Rod had returned to the Rangers, the rumor in the sports world was that he was going to become a Yankee. On February 15, 2004, the story broke: Texas was trading A-Rod for Yankee Alfonso Soriano. Rangers owner Tom Hicks had made the decision. "My baseball experts gave me their advice," Hicks said, "and it was that we can build a championship team faster here in Texas by doing this trade today."

For A-Rod, becoming a Yankee was an incredible feeling. He was joining the most successful team in baseball history. A-Rod accepted the position of third baseman, and Derek Jeter would continue on as shortstop. "I think we will make a great tag team," A-Rod said during the press conference at Yankee Stadium announcing the trade. "Derek is a 'great' here. . . . I want to learn from him and play under his leadership."

 "I look at it as a new challenge. I achieved just about everything personally at shortstop. Now it's time to win. I've always thought of myself as a team player. Playing third base is the ultimate team move."

—A-Rod, on switching to third base

February 16, 2004

Like it or not, Big Apple's best place for baseball's best player to shine

From the Pages of
USA TODAY

Turn a deaf ear to the Pittsburghs and Kansas Cities screaming bloody murder over this union of embarrassing contract and embarrassing payroll. Alex Rodriguez to the Yankees, ladies and gentlemen, is good for baseball. You can't have the Michael Jordan of your sport playing for the Los Angeles Clippers forever.

One way or another, Rodriguez had to escape to New York. Baseball couldn't afford to keep him locked up in the Texas wastelands, where high school football will always be bigger than the ALDS.

Rodriguez lugs along a chunk of his $252 million contract bigger than the courthouse behind Yankee Stadium's right-center wall. You can already hear the screams from baseball's cheap seats, where A-Rod's monthly wage equals half a team's operating budget.

A-Rod was so desperate to get out of Texas that he approached Bud Selig at Sammy Sosa's November birthday party in the Dominican Republic to let the

In March A-Rod was amazed by the spectacle before the Yankees' first spring training game. Fireworks, parachutists, and Yankee greats including Reggie Jackson, Whitey Ford, and Yogi Berra were all a part of the lavish pregame celebration. A-Rod had to pinch himself. "When you see all the [Yankee] Hall of Famers lining up," he said, "it's hard not to get caught up in the moment."

After the game against the Philadelphia Phillies, which the Yankees won 7–5, A-Rod said that playing for the Yankees felt like a dream.

commissioner know he was extremely unhappy with the Rangers. When the possible Manny Ramirez trade arose, Selig figured Boston was an ideal landing place.

It didn't happen, thanks to union leaders who exist to rain on parades. But neither Donald Fehr nor Gene Orza stood in Steinbrenner's way. The Yankees didn't want to devalue A-Rod's landmark contract; they only wanted the Rangers to pay their fair share of it and to accept Alfonso Soriano as a reward for being so kind.

Rodriguez and Derek Jeter, old flames who've had more breakups and makeups than Ben and J-Lo, will remain in each other's arms until someone reminds Jeter about those nasty things A-Rod said about him before they started making commercials together. For the time being, nobody's asking why A-Rod is going to third when Jeter is the second-best shortstop of the two. That question will come after the honeymoon.

The Mets had their chance after losing the 2000 World Series to the Yankees. Rodriguez was born a Mets fan and wanted to go head-to-head with Jeter for prince-of-the-city rights. Instead of making him an offer, Mets owner Fred Wilpon proved he doesn't have the stomach for the big-market fight. He told A-Rod where to stuff his hometown dreams. Sure looks like a brilliant move now.

The Red Sox at least gave it the ol' college try. In the end, they did beat the Yanks to Curt Schilling. If baseball's pitching-is-everything principles hold up in another ALCS, Schilling will be more important to the Red Sox than A-Rod will be to the Yanks.

But there's six months of Arena Baseball to play before anyone finds out. A-Rod, Jeter, Jason Giambi and Gary Sheffield. The Yankees will score, score, score, and hope they can get to Mariano Rivera.

—Ian O'Connor

"When I was rounding third, I asked myself, 'Where am I?' I felt like I was in Disney World," he told reporters.

"On Another Planet"

A-Rod was thrilled and awed to be part of the legendary Yankees, and he wrote about it in a cover story for *ESPN the Magazine*. "I honestly feel like I'm on another planet," he wrote. "You go from three straight years of last place to this, and it's like breathing a different kind of air."

On April 8, Alex played his first game at Yankee Stadium. He scored a run, helping the Yanks beat the Chicago White Sox 3–1. He was cheered by fans, who were happy to have him on board as their third baseman.

"I like playing at the Stadium. I like hitting at the Stadium. I feel like I'm home."

—Alex, on playing at Yankee Stadium

But it was a much different story when the team headed to Fenway Park on April 16 to play the Boston Red Sox. During batting practice, one Red Sox fan yelled to him, "Hey, A-Rod! What's it like to be Jeter's backup?"—implying that as third baseman, A-Rod was less important than star shortstop Derek Jeter. And every time A-Rod came to the plate during the game, the Boston fans booed. "It was pretty intense

Talking strategy: Alex talks with shortstop Derek Jeter *(left)* before a game against the Boston Red Sox in April 2004 at Yankee Stadium.

IN FOCUS

Lucky 13

Starting in high school, A-Rod always wore number 3 on his baseball uniform. But he couldn't wear 3 as a Yankee because the Yankees had retired the number (no longer used it) after the legendary hitter Babe Ruth (also number 3) left the team. So A-Rod added a 1 to Ruth's number and chose number 13 for his Yankees jersey. Thirteen also happened to be the number worn by one of A-Rod's childhood idols, Dan Marino of the Miami Dolphins football team.

out there," he said afterward. "The fans here are always intense and rabid. Tonight was as loud as I've heard it."

Though he tried hard not to be affected by all the negativity toward him, Alex struggled in Boston. In the series against the Red Sox, he went 1 for 17 (one hit in 17 at bats), and his batting average dropped to .160. When he grounded out during a game on April 17, he slammed down his helmet. Later, A-Rod said it felt good to vent. "Sometimes you need to let it out, let the frustration out," he said. "When you've been stinking up the place like I have lately, the focus is definitely to let out some emotion."

Things started turning around for A-Rod when he hit his second homer as a Yankee during an April 21 game against the White Sox. Then on May 4, in a game against the Oakland A's, he hit his 350th career homer. He became the 70th player to reach that goal and the youngest in major-league history (28 years, 282 days). "This is my biggest hit as a Yankee," he said.

Yankees manager Joe Torre admired A-Rod's sense of team spirit. "He's a very respectful guy," he said. "The one thing is, I don't care how big a star he is, or how much money he makes. . . . He's a hard worker."

"He is baseball twenty-four hours a day. When we were kids, he'd make me meet him at the park at 5:30 in the morning. I'd be half asleep, and he'd be like, 'O.K., drills!'"

—Gui Soccaras, longtime A-Rod pal

Historic Loss

In the second game of a September 29 doubleheader against the Minnesota Twins, A-Rod powered a two-run triple in the seventh inning and then smacked his 36th homer of the season. "This is the best I've felt all year," said Alex. The Yankees were feeling pretty good too. With several key hits, A-Rod helped them win all three games of a three-game series against the Minnesota Twins.

When the regular season ended, the Yankees were in first place in their division, the AL East, with a 101–61 record. In the ALDS, the Yankees faced the Minnesota Twins. The Yankees had beat the Twins just five days earlier, so they had a lot of confidence going into the series. But in game one, the Twins beat the Yanks on their home turf—Yankee Stadium. Game two was tied after nine innings, and by the bottom of the twelfth, the Twins were leading 6–5. A-Rod came to bat with one out and runners on first and second. He smacked a line drive to left-center field, and the ball bounced over the fence for a ground-rule double. One runner scored, tying the game. A-Rod was still on second base later in the inning when Derek Jeter scored the winning run. The series headed to Minnesota for games three and four. The Yankees dominated game three, winning 8–4, and then battled for 11 innings to win game four, 6–5, with A-Rod scoring the winning run.

In the ALCS, the Yanks' opponents were their historic rivals—the Boston Red Sox. New York started off strong, winning games one and two. After winning game three 19–8, thanks in part to an A-Rod home run, the Yankees seemed sure to sweep the series. No team had ever

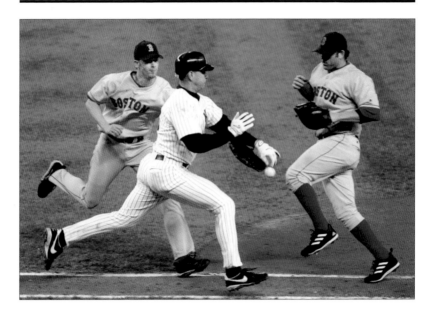

Whatever it takes: Alex swats at the glove of Red Sox pitcher Bronson Arroyo *(left)* as he runs to first in the eighth inning of game six of the 2004 ALCS. Alex was called out by the umpire for interfering with the play.

blown a three-game lead to lose a seven-game post-season series. But Boston won games four and five in extra innings. Then the Red Sox won a close game six before blowing out the Yankees in game seven by a score of 10–3.

"This is obviously crushing for us," A-Rod told reporters about the devastating ALCS loss. "I don't have words for

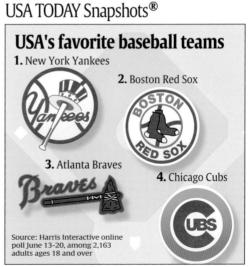

USA TODAY Snapshots®

USA's favorite baseball teams

1. New York Yankees

2. Boston Red Sox

3. Atlanta Braves

4. Chicago Cubs

Source: Harris Interactive online poll June 13–20, among 2,163 adults ages 18 and over

By Matt Young and Sam Ward, USA TODAY, 2011

the disappointment." The Yankees couldn't pull themselves together after three devastating losses, and the Red Sox won game seven and the pennant.

The Boston Red Sox went on to sweep the St. Louis Cardinals in the 2004 World Series, claiming their first world championship in 86 years.

Alex felt he and the Yankees could have accomplished more. "The fact that I haven't won a championship bothers me," he said. "Until I do, I will not sleep or be comfortable with my career."

Mr. 400

A-Rod was excited about a new development in his life. On November 18, 2004, his wife, Cynthia, gave birth to their first child, daughter Natasha Alexander. Becoming a father was thrilling to A-Rod. He wanted to help Natasha grow and learn. Most important, he wanted to be there to nurture her.

On the field, A-Rod was doing well in 2005. In an April 27 game against the Los Angeles Angels (formerly known as the

Family: Cynthia Rodriguez and daughter Natasha watch Alex work out with the Yankees during spring training in 2007.

Anaheim Angels), he hit three homers in his first three at bats and helped his team to a 12–4 victory. "Tonight was one of those magical nights. It felt like I was in the clouds—you just don't want it to end," he said of his performance before 36,328 wildly cheering fans at Yankee Stadium. "I've hit three home runs twice before, but nothing feels as special as this, doing it in New York, doing it in the pinstripes [Yankees uniform]." He also became only the 11th major league-player with 10 or more RBIs in a game.

In early June, A-Rod admitted something personal to reporters. He said he had been seeing a therapist to resolve issues from his childhood. The most difficult problem he had faced was his father abandoning the family when Alex was so young. Alex wanted kids everywhere to know that even a sports star can use help sometimes. "What's hap-

pening with little kids in today's generation is a lot of suicide, a lot of mental problems going on, and a lot of it is because they think therapy is a real bad thing," he said. "And it's not. And that's why I came out and said it's been very helpful in my personal life."

Just days later, on June 8, A-Rod reached a milestone when he powered his 400th home run against the Milwaukee Brewers. By the end of July, he was batting .318 and was happy about his position with the team.

"It's good to have him up near the top of the lineup

Number 400: Alex slams home run number 400 on June 8, 2005.

IN F⌖CUS

Give a Hand

In the spring of 2005, A-Rod and his wife, Cynthia, donated $200,000 to a children's mental health center in Washington Heights, the New York City neighborhood where A-Rod was born.

because he can set things up for guys like me and [Gary Sheffield]," designated hitter Jason Giambi said about A-Rod. "And I've always said, every time he comes up he's in scoring position."

Hopes were high when the Yankees faced the Los Angeles Angels in the best-of-five-game ALDS. After winning the first game with a score of 4–2 and losing the next two, the Yankees forced a fifth game when they defeated the Angels 3–2 on October 9. Ultimately, the Yankees lost game five and squelched their chance of competing against the Chicago White Sox in the 2005 ALCS.

A-Rod was especially upset about his performance in the ALDS. He'd hit 2 for 15 with a .133 average and no RBIs during the series. "I played great baseball all year and I played like a dog for five days," Alex told reporters. The third baseman even apologized to Yankees coaches for grounding out into a double play in the ninth inning of game five.

But despite his lackluster postseason play, A-Rod had still had a fantastic sophomore season as a Yankee. He had a .321 average, 130 RBIs, 194 hits, 48 home runs, and 21 stolen bases. And once he let the crushing disappointment of the ALDS loss settle in, he felt optimistic about the 2006 season. "I still believe we're the best team in baseball," he said. "I'll always think that. You can't question our effort." The same can be said for A-Rod, who always gives his all.

Although Alex Rodriguez didn't play in the 2005 World Series, he still received a special honor there. On October 26, before game four of the series, A-Rod walked on the field at the Houston Astrodome to be named a member of the "Latino Legends" baseball team, along with such greats as the late Roberto Clemente, Juan Marichal, and Rod Carew. A-Rod was proud to be admired as one of the best Latino players in baseball. "It's just a tremendous honor," he said. "It's a treat. It's pretty special."

After the season, White Sox manager Ozzie Guillen made the case for why A-Rod should win the MVP award over the other leading contender, Red Sox designated hitter David Ortiz: "[A-Rod] steals bases, goes from first to third, makes all the plays on defense, gets the big hits," Guillen said. "He can beat you so many [more] ways than Ortiz." Yankees teammate Randy Johnson added, "Alex is the MVP. I've seen him save countless games with his defense and win countless games with his offense."

The good news came on November 14, 2005, when 30-year-old Alex Rodriguez was indeed named American League Most Valuable Player. Yankees owner George Steinbrenner praised his MVP. "A-Rod demonstrates the talent, hard work, and dedication of a true winner," he said. But A-Rod admitted, "I would certainly trade [David Ortiz's 2004] World Series championship for this MVP trophy. [Winning the World Series is] the only reason I play baseball."

Latino legend: Alex waves to the crowd while walking onto the field as part of the Latino Legends baseball team in 2005.

Another record: Derek Jeter congratulates Alex on his three-run homer against the Blue Jays in 2006. It was Alex's 2,000th hit and 450th home run of his career.

Historic Slugger

■■■■

With his second MVP award under his belt, Alex was ready to continue his pursuit of a World Series title in 2006. By July 1 the Yankees had a record of 45–33, but they were tied with the Blue Jays and trailed the Red Sox for the division lead by four games. As usual, the AL East was one of the toughest divisions in baseball.

In a game against the Blue Jays in Toronto on July 21, pitcher A. J. Burnett threw a ball that A-Rod launched into the outfield bleachers. This was the 2,000th hit of A-Rod's remarkable career and his 450th home run. With this blast, A-Rod became the youngest player to ever hit 450 home runs. He was six days shy of his 31st birthday. Unfortunately, the Blue Jays won the game, 7–3. "Four hundred fifty is something I'm proud of and 2,000 at the same time, it's kind of unique," Rodriguez said. "Unfortunately, we couldn't do it with a win, but I'm still going to enjoy it."

A-Rod had another good season at the plate with a .290 batting average, 35 home runs, and 121 RBIs. The Yankees played well as a

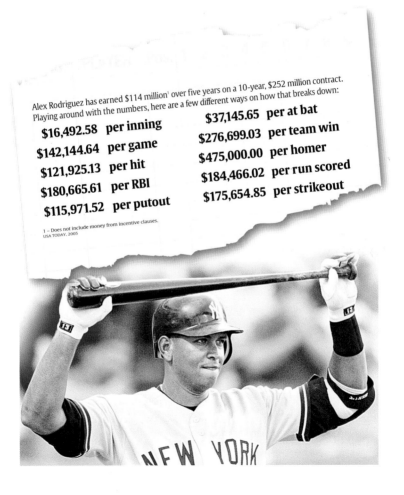

Alex Rodriguez has earned $114 million[1] over five years on a 10-year, $252 million contract. Playing around with the numbers, here are a few different ways on how that breaks down:

$16,492.58 **per inning**

$142,144.64 **per game**

$121,925.13 **per hit**

$180,665.61 **per RBI**

$115,971.52 **per putout**

$37,145.65 **per at bat**

$276,699.03 **per team win**

$475,000.00 **per homer**

$184,466.02 **per run scored**

$175,654.85 **per strikeout**

1 – Does not include money from incentive clauses.
USA TODAY, 2005

team and finished the season with 97 wins, good enough for first place in the AL East. The Yankees faced the Detroit Tigers in the 2006 ALDS. New York started strong, winning game one by a score of 8–4. From there the team faltered, however, losing the next three games and the series. And once again, Alex played poorly in the postseason with only one hit in 14 at bats. "I don't know how to explain it," Rodriguez said. "I hit some balls hard that got caught. Overall, I wish I could have done better."

A-Rod and the Yankees began the 2007 season with confidence but quickly found themselves trying to catch up in the AL East. On April 23 against Tampa Bay, the team lost its fourth-straight game and fell to a record of 8–10. Even though the season was just a few weeks old, the Yankees found themselves in fourth place and four games behind the first-place Red Sox.

New York was struggling, but A-Rod seemed to have found his groove. In the game against Tampa Bay on April 23, Alex hit his 14th home run of the season in just 18 games. No player in baseball history had hit so many home runs in so few games to begin a season. "The guy's on fire, and I hope he keeps it up," teammate Johnny Damon said. "The whole team is rallying around him. We can't wait until the next time he comes up." Personal success aside, Alex knew the team would have to start winning soon if they wanted to reach the postseason for the 13th year in a row.

To 500 and Beyond

In a game against the Royals on August 4, A-Rod came to bat against Kyle Davies and smashed the first pitch he saw into the left-field seats for a home run. With this blast, A-Rod became the youngest player in baseball history to hit 500 home runs. He was 32 years and eight days old. Alex was glad to reach the 500 home run mark, and he was even happier to do it in his home stadium. "To do it at home and to wear this beautiful uniform that I appreciate and respect so much, it's special," A-Rod said. "New York is a special place."

Alex didn't slow down after his home run milestone in August, and 2007 proved to be one of his best seasons statistically. A-Rod had a .314 batting average and belted 54 home runs, and was named AL MVP for the third time. But the season ended in familiar fashion for the Yankees. Once again, Alex didn't play well in the postseason, and New York was beaten by the Indians in the ALDS in four games.

 A-Rod doesn't take a limousine to home games like some players. He prefers to drive himself. "[Driving is] my personal time to prepare for the game or wind down from it," he says.

In December 2007, former U.S. senator George Mitchell released a report that accused 89 former and current baseball players of using performance-enhancing drugs (PEDs). These drugs are illegal, but some players used them to throw harder, hit the ball farther, or recover more quickly from injury. The report did not accuse A-Rod of taking drugs, but some people still suspected him because of his amazing ability to hit home runs.

After the release of George Mitchell's report, A-Rod agreed to be interviewed by CBS News. Reporter Katie Couric asked Alex, "For the record, have you ever used steroids, human growth hormone or any other performance-enhancing substance?" A-Rod's answer was short but clear: "No," he said.

A-Rod missed the first month of the 2008 season with a leg injury, but his time off the field was kept busy by personal matters. On April 21, Cynthia gave birth to the couple's second child, Ella Alexander, in Miami. Yet despite the new addition to the family, A-Rod's marriage was in turmoil. Cynthia filed for divorce on July 7. She stated in court papers that Alex had "emotionally abandoned his wife and children."

Events on the baseball field were also disappointing for Alex in 2008. When he returned to the Yankees lineup in May, the team was in fourth place in the AL East with a 14–16 record. New York could not catch up. When the season ended, the Yankees were in third place and out of the playoffs for the first time in 14 years. Even so, Alex had another good year with a .302 batting average, 35 home runs, and 103 RBIs.

Ups and Downs

The offseason brought more problems for Alex. Rumors had been swirling in the baseball world that he had failed a test for PEDs back in 2003. The results of this test were supposed to be secret, but the information was leaked to reporters. In an interview with ESPN in February of 2009, A-Rod admitted to taking PEDs during his three seasons with the Texas Rangers (2001–2003). "I did take a banned substance. And for that, I am very sorry and deeply regretful," Alex admitted. He said his illegal drug use was behind him, but many felt his admission cast a shadow over his great career.

The 2009 season began in much the same way as 2008. This time, Alex was unable to play due to an injury in his hip. When he was finally able to return to the New York lineup on May 8, he smacked the first pitch he saw over the fence in centerfield for a home run. A-Rod seemed relieved to be back and playing well after the injury and the scandal of the offseason. "It was nice to do what I do best," he said after the game, "which is play baseball."

A-Rod played well throughout 2009 and ended the season with 30 home runs and 100 RBIs. Even better, the Yankees crushed their AL East competition to finish eight games in front of the second-place Red Sox. New York was headed back to the playoffs. Alex was determined to put his postseason failures of the past behind him.

The Yankees beat up on the Minnesota Twins in the first game of the 2009 ALDS, winning 7–2. In game two, the Twins were ahead 3–1 in the ninth inning when A-Rod stepped to the plate and crushed the ball over the outfield fence for a two-run home run to tie the game. The Yankees eventually won the game, 4–3. The slugger homered again in game three, a 4–1 Yankees victory.

Alex and his team continued to play well in the ALCS against the Angels, and the Yankees took the series in six games. New York was headed to the World Series to take on the Philadelphia Phillies! Through the first two rounds of the playoffs, A-Rod was hitting an astonishing .437 with five home runs and 12 RBIs. But to become a true postseason hero, Alex would have to continue to mash the ball in the World Series.

Fall Classic

The Yankees and the Phillies split the first two games of the 2009 World Series. The Phillies struck early in game three with three runs in the second inning. The pressure was on the New York offense to stage a comeback. When A-Rod came to the plate in the fourth inning with team-mate Mark Teixeira on base, A-Rod had yet to re-cord a hit in the World Series—but that was about to change. Alex swung at the second pitch and sent it deep into right field. The ball appeared to bounce off the top of the wall and back onto the field, allow-ing Teixeira to run all the way home. But Yankees manager Joe Girardi came

Playing defense: Alex throws to first for an out during game one of the 2009 World Series.

out to argue the call with the umpires. He thought the ball had gone over the wall for a home run before bouncing back onto the field. After looking at the video replay, the umpires decided that Girardi was right. The ball had bounced off a camera above the outfield fence for a home run! New York had cut the Philadelphia lead to just one run.

The Yankees added more runs in the fifth, sixth, seventh, and eighth innings, and won game three, 8–5. A-Rod had the game-winning RBI in the Yankees' game four victory. Then he knocked in three more runs in game five. It wasn't enough, though, as the Phillies stayed alive in the series with an 8–6 victory. Alex drew two walks and had a hit in game six, a 7–3 New York victory. A-Rod and the Yankees were world champions! "We're going to enjoy it, and we're going to party!" Alex said after the game.

Alex finally had the World Series victory that he'd wanted for so long, and he'd been a huge part of his team's success. Overall, he had

A team on top: Alex *(number 13)* and his Yankees teammates celebrate their 2009 World Series win on November 4, 2009.

a .365 batting average with six home runs and 18 RBIs in the 2009 postseason. A-Rod's family problems and the drug issues that had plagued him before the season seemed like distant memories.

The Yankees were flying high and eager for the beginning of the 2010 season. A-Rod was healthy, and the team got out to a fast start. By July 1, New York had a firm grip on first place in the AL East with a 48–30 record. A-Rod's life off the field was also heating up. Since his divorce in 2008 he had tried to keep his personal life out of the media, but rumors started linking A-Rod to famous actress Cameron

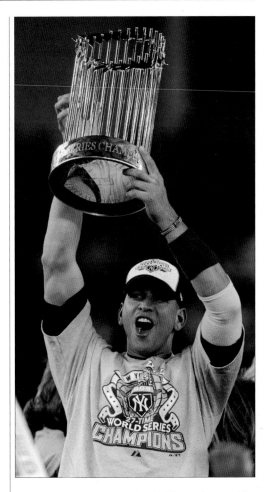

World Series champ: Alex holds up the World Series championship trophy following the Yankee's 2009 win.

Diaz. For her part, Diaz also tried to downplay the relationship. When asked about Alex in an interview with *Harper's Bazaar* in July 2010, Diaz played coy, saying only that "I grew up with the Dodgers, but now I'm a Yankees fan."

On August 4, the three-year anniversary of his 500th home run, A-Rod reached another career milestone when he hit a blast over the

August 5, 2010

Can A-Rod catch Bonds?

From the Pages of USA TODAY Now that Alex Rodriguez has 600 home runs in his rearview mirror, how many might the New York Yankees third baseman expect to hit?

"Six hundred home runs—that's ridiculous. That's a lot of home runs, man," teammate Nick Swisher says. "But 700, eight, nine, 1,000—I don't know.

"He's such a talented player, and with the way he takes care of himself, anything's possible."

Rodriguez turned 35 on July 27. No other player has reached 600 before his 36th birthday, although Yankees icon Babe Ruth did it in fewer games—2,044 to 2,227.

But the numbers indicate that Rodriguez's body might already be in decline and that catching leader Barry Bonds (762), let alone becoming the first player to reach 800, might not be as easy as it once appeared.

For one thing, Rodriguez is dealing with a surgically repaired hip that limited him to 124 games in 2009 when he hit 30 home runs, his lowest total in the last 12 seasons.

This year, homers are down across baseball and Rodriguez has hit 17, putting him on pace for 26 at season's end.

Early last month, Hall of Famer Reggie Jackson, a special adviser for the Yankees, predicted Rodriguez "is going to hit 800 home runs."

outfield fence in the first inning of a game against Toronto's Shaun Marcum. With this smash, A-Rod became the seventh player in MLB history to hit 600 home runs. (Jim Thome joined the 600 home run club in 2011.) Coming just eight days after his 35th birthday, Alex was the youngest slugger to reach this mark. People began to wonder if he would someday challenge the all-time home run record held by Barry

Later in the month, Jackson backed off just a bit.

"He's got to stay healthy," Jackson said. "You don't know how long his hip is going to stay healthy. Right now, I don't know if he's going to make 800.

"With the pace he had before the hip surgery, I would say yes. But I have my doubts now. It would really (depend) on how he physically holds up, because he'd have to hit 35 a year (to do it in six seasons)—and he was putting up 40 a year, 50 a year."

Rodriguez, who hit 57 homers for the Texas Rangers in 2002—the middle year of a three-year period in which he admitted using banned performance-enhancing drugs—and 54 for the Yankees when he won his third American League MVP Award in 2007, has seven years remaining on a 10-year, $275 million contract. From 2001 to 2007, he averaged 47 homers. He's totaled 82 homers in the three seasons since.

"(No. 600) is definitely a special number," Rodriguez said Wednesday. "I'm certainly proud of it and will treasure it. Many, many years from today, I will be able to reflect a lot better."

Besides, Rodriguez struggled through a 12-game drought to hit the milestone home run. Going forward, he says he would rather focus on passing individuals than round numbers.

"The real milestone is when you start passing the all-time greats," Rodriguez said. "As long as it doesn't have a zero at the end, I think I'm going to be OK."

Teammates seem to think Rodriguez has plenty of spring left.

"For Alex to (reach 600) at a young age and for a milestone like this not to be enough for him just shows his competitiveness and his drive to be the best," says first baseman Mark Teixeira, who leads the Yankees with 23 home runs. "I hope to be standing here in five or six years and have Alex get to 800—and I think everyone expects that for him."

—Seth Livingstone

Bonds (762). "It took me three years to the day to hit 100, so that's not really on my radar right now," Rodriguez said. "That's something I'll revisit in two or three years."

For the second year in a row, the Yankees swept the Twins in the first round of the playoffs. New York moved on to face A-Rod's former team, the Texas Rangers, in the 2010 ALCS. The Yankees won games

Elite league: Alex hits home run number 600. Including Alex, only eight players have reached this home run milestone.

one and five, but Texas won games two, three, and four. New York was on the brink of elimination in game six and trailed the Rangers by five runs when Alex came to the plate in the bottom of the ninth inning. He struck out looking. Alex knew that the fans and players in Texas had still not forgiven him for admitting he'd taken PEDs during his years with the team. "I'm the last guy up there," A-Rod said. "I'm sure that made it a little sweeter for them."

Living Legend

After the disappointment of losing to the Rangers in the 2010 ALCS, A-Rod was eager to change his focus during the offseason. His relationship with Cameron Diaz continued to make news. The couple even attended Super Bowl XLV together, and Diaz was photographed playfully feeding popcorn to Alex.

The slugger also focused on his body before the start of the 2011 season. Alex wanted to avoid the injuries that had plagued him in recent years, so he worked hard to increase his flexibility. He also lost about 10

A new romance: Alex and actress Cameron Diaz attend an event at the Latin Baseball Hall of Fame in the Dominican Republic in 2010.

pounds (4.5 kg) and lowered his body fat to 9 percent. "I just feel lighter," A-Rod said during spring training in March. "I feel quicker on my feet."

By midseason the Yankees had a firm grip on the AL East that they would not give up. When the season ended on September 28, New York had a six-game lead on Tampa Bay for the division crown. In the ALDS against the Detroit Tigers, he had only two hits for a batting average of .111. Many of A-Rod's teammates also performed poorly at the plate, and the Tigers won game five in New York to take the series. For the second year in a row, Alex struck out to end the final game of the year for the Yankees. "This one especially stings," Alex said. "We should have won, and we had opportunities there late."

Winning the World Series has been A-Rod's quest since he started playing baseball as a little boy in the Dominican Republic. This goal has driven him to succeed in the major leagues. Since his team's world championship in 2009, Alex has continued to work hard both at the plate and in the field. "We must always strive to do the right thing," he once wrote. "In my case, that means playing hard and honorably. In doing so, I honor all those people who have supported me throughout my life."

CAREER STATISTICS

Year	Team	Avg	G	AB	Runs	Hits	2B	3B	HR	RBI	SB
1994	SEA	.204	17	54	4	11	0	0	0	2	3
1995	SEA	.232	48	142	15	33	6	2	5	19	4
1996	SEA	.358	146	601	141	215	54	1	36	123	15
1997	SEA	.300	141	587	100	176	40	3	23	84	29
1998	SEA	.310	161	686	123	213	35	5	42	124	46
1999	SEA	.285	129	502	110	143	25	0	42	111	21
2000	SEA	.316	148	554	134	175	34	2	41	132	15
2001	TEX	.318	162	632	133	201	34	1	52	135	18
2002	TEX	.300	162	624	125	187	27	2	57	142	9
2003	TEX	.298	161	607	124	181	30	6	47	118	17
2004	NYY	.286	155	601	112	172	24	2	36	106	28
2005	NYY	.321	162	605	124	194	29	1	48	130	21
2006	NYY	.290	154	572	113	166	26	1	35	121	15
2007	NYY	.314	158	583	143	183	31	0	54	156	24
2008	NYY	.302	138	510	104	154	33	0	35	103	18
2009	NYY	.286	124	444	78	127	17	1	30	100	14
2010	NYY	.270	137	522	74	141	29	2	30	125	4
2011	NYY	.276	99	373	67	103	21	0	16	62	4

(Totals—Avg: .302; G: 2,402; AB: 9,199; Runs: 1,824; Hits: 2,775; 2B: 495; 3B: 29; HR: 629; RBI: 1,893; SB: 305)

Key: Avg: batting average; G: games; AB: at bats; 2B: doubles; 3B: triples; HR: home runs; RBI: runs batted in; SB: stolen bases

GLOSSARY

American League Championship Series (ALCS): a set of games played at the end of the baseball season between the two top American League teams. The team that wins four games goes to the World Series to play the winner of the National League Championship Series.

American League Division Series (ALDS): two sets of games played at the end of the baseball season between the three American League division winners and the team with the best record that did not win its division. Teams that win three games go to the ALCS to play the winner of the other ALDS.

draft: a system for selecting new players for professional sports teams

Major League Baseball (MLB): the top group of professional men's baseball teams in North America, divided into the American League and the National League

minor leagues: groups of teams in which players improve their skills and prepare to move to the majors

performance-enhancing drugs (PEDs): drugs used to increase muscle mass and strength, as well as to recover more quickly from injury. MLB bans the use of PEDs.

rookie: a first-year player

scouts: people who judge the skills of players. Scouts work for individual teams and help them decide whom to draft.

shortstop: a player who plays in the field between second base and third base

spring training: a time from February through early April when baseball teams train for the season

SOURCE NOTES

6   *Houston Chronicle*, "A-Rod Hits 400th in Yankee Revival," June 9, 2005, 7.

6   *Times* (London), "Rodriguez Reaches Milestone," June 10, 2005, 91.

8   Alex Rodriguez and Greg Brown, *Alex Rodriguez: Hit a Grand Slam!* (Dallas: Taylor Publishing Co., 1998), 38.

10   Matt Christopher, *On the Field with . . . Alex Rodriguez* (New York: Little, Brown and Co., 2002), 3.

10   Ibid., 4.

10   Rodriguez and Brown, *Hit a Grand Slam!*, 10.

10   Ibid., 13.

11   Ibid., 12.

12   Jim Gallagher, *Alex Rodriguez* (Bear, DE: Mitchell Lane Publishers, 2000), 13–14.

12   James Fitzgerald, *A-Rod: Major League Hero* (New York: Penguin Group, 2004), 23.

15   Christopher, *On the Field with . . . Alex Rodriguez*, 23.

15   Ibid.

17   Ibid., 24.

17   Ibid., 25–26.

17   Rodriguez and Brown, *Hit a Grand Slam!*, 25.

18   Christopher, *On the Field with . . . Alex Rodriguez*, 25.

18   Ibid., 25–26.

18   Ibid., 28.

18   Rodriguez and Brown, *Hit a Grand Slam!*, 24.

20   Ibid., 26.

22   Fitzgerald, *A-Rod*, 32.

23   Rodriguez and Brown, *Hit a Grand Slam!*, 28.

24–25   Ibid., 36.

25   Ibid., 37.

25   Ibid., 45.

26–27   Fitzgerald, *A-Rod*, 38.

29   Rodriguez and Brown, *Hit a Grand Slam!*, 29.

29–30   Christopher, *On the Field with . . . Alex Rodriguez*, 49.

33   Ibid., 59.

34   Fitzgerald, *A-Rod*, 46.

34 Rodriguez and Brown, *Hit a Grand Slam!*, 30.

36 Ibid., 31.

36 Christopher, *On the Field with . . . Alex Rodriguez*, 71.

36 Gallagher, *Alex Rodriguez*, 23.

36 Rodriguez and Brown, *Hit a Grand Slam!*, 31.

37 Ibid., 32.

37 Christopher, *On the Field with . . . Alex Rodriguez*, 85.

38 Rodriguez and Brown, *Hit a Grand Slam!*, 75.

38 Ibid., 32.

38 Ibid., 33.

39 Gallagher, *Alex Rodriguez*, 30.

39 Rodriguez and Brown, *Hit a Grand Slam!*, 33.

40–41 Gallagher, *Alex Rodriguez*, 34.

41 Fitzgerald, *A-Rod*, 61.

44 Gallagher, *Alex Rodriguez*, 36.

45 Michael Bradley, *Alex Rodriguez* (New York: Benchmark Books, 2005), 26.

45 Rodriguez and Brown, *Hit a Grand Slam!*, 36.

46 Christopher, *On the Field with . . . Alex Rodriguez*, 23.

46 Gallagher, *Alex Rodriguez*, 39.

46 Ibid., 41.

47 Rodriguez and Brown, *Hit a Grand Slam!*, 37.

47 Christopher, *On the Field with . . . Alex Rodriguez*, 98–99.

49 Ibid., 40.

49 Gallagher, *Alex Rodriguez*, 49.

51 Rodriguez and Brown, *Hit a Grand Slam!*, 38.

51 Fitzgerald, *A-Rod*, 69.

54 Gallagher, *Alex Rodriguez*, 61.

56–57 Bradley, *Alex Rodriguez*, 33.

59 Gallagher, *Alex Rodriguez*, 59.

59 Ibid.

59 Christopher, *On the Field with . . . Alex Rodriguez*, 109.

62 Bradley, *Alex Rodriguez*, 34.

62 Gallagher, *Alex Rodriguez*, 58.

65 Fitzgerald, *A-Rod*, 75.

67 Christopher, *On the Field with . . . Alex Rodriguez*, 114.

68 Bradley, *Alex Rodriguez*, 37.

70   Fitzgerald, *A-Rod*, 85–86.

70   Christopher, *On the Field with . . . Alex Rodriguez*, 119.

70   Ibid.

71   Bradley, *Alex Rodriguez*, 40.

71   Ibid.

72   Fitzgerald, *A-Rod*, 91.

75   Christopher, *On the Field with . . . Alex Rodriguez*, 123.

77   Fitzgerald, *A-Rod*, 109.

77   Ibid., 112.

77   Ibid., 120.

77   Tom Verducci, "New York State of Mind," *Sports Illustrated*, June 6, 2005, 38.

78   Ibid., 128.

79   Ronald Blum, "Rodriguez Makes Spring Training Debut for Yankees," Associated Press, March 5, 2004.

79   Chris De Luca, "Alex in Wonderland," *Chicago Sun-Times*, April 8, 2004, 133.

80   Verducci, "New York State of Mind," 38.

80   Ben Walker, "A-Rod, Yankees Renew Baseball's Best Rivalry at Fenway Park," Associated Press, April 17, 2004.

80–81   Nick Cafardo, "A-Rod Introduced to Rivalry," *Boston Globe*, April 17, 2004, E6.

81   Nick Cafardo, "Rodriguez Says He'll Work It Out," *Boston Globe*, April 18, 2004, D12.

81   Associated Press, "A-Rod Hits 350th Homer; Yanks Tie AL East," May 5, 2004.

81   Mark Gonzales, "City Slicker; A-Rod Slowly Warms to a New York State of Mind," *Arizona Republic*, June 15, 2004, 1C.

82   Verducci, "New York State of Mind," 38.

82   Dave Caldwell, "Division Is Almost in Yanks' Hands," *New York Times*, September 30, 2004, D1.

83–84   Kathleen O'Brien, "A-Rod Turns into A-Clod in ALCS," *Fort Worth Star-Telegram*, October 22, 2004.

84   Jack Curry, "Rodriguez Is Haunted by Yanks' Collapse," *New York Times*, November 14, 2004, D1.

85   Howie Rumberg, "A-Rod Homers Three Times in Yankees Win," Associated Press, April 27, 2005.

85 *Pittsburgh Post-Gazette*, "A-Rod Remains True to Game," June 4, 2005, E2.

85–86 Mike Anthony, "Satisfying Turn for A-Rod; Puts to Rest Nightmares of First Season with Yankees," *Hartford (CT) Courant*, October 2, 2005, E15.

86 Joel Sherman, "Money Bawl: Yanks' Big Stars Fizzled in Clutch," *New York Post*, October 11, 2005, 98.

86 Lisa Olson, "A-Rod Wilts in Dog Days," *New York Daily News*, October 11, 2005, 67.

87 Sam Borden, "As a 'Legend,' A-Rod Gets to Series at Last," *New York Daily News*, October 27, 2005, 81.

87 Tom Verducci, "Who's the Man?" *Sports Illustrated*, October 10, 2005, 48.

87 Anthony, "Satisfying Turn for A-Rod."

87 Ronald Blum, "Rodriguez Beats Ortiz to Win Second MVP in Three Seasons," Associated Press, November 14, 2005.

87 Ibid.

89 Alex Rodriguez, quoted in "A-Rod Youngest to 450 HRs but Error Helps Sink Yanks," ESPN.com, July 21, 2006, http://scores.espn.go.com/mlb/recap?gameId=260721114 (September 15, 2011).

90 Alex Rodriguez, quoted in "Yanks' Postseason Ends in Game 4," MLB.com, October 7, 2006, http://newyork.yankees.mlb.com/news/article.jsp?ymd=20061007&content_id=1703772&vkey=recap&fext=.jsp&c_id=nyy (September 29, 2011).

90 Johnny Damon, quoted in "Rodriguez's Record Can't Improve Yankees,'" *nytimes.com*, April 24, 2007, http://www.nytimes.com/2007/04/24/sports/baseball/24yankees.html (September 29, 2011).

90 Alex Rodriguez, quoted in "A-Rod Belts Historic 500th Homer," *MLB.com*, August 4, 2007, http://mlb.mlb.com/news/article.jsp?ymd=20070804&content_id=2129099&vkey=news_nyy&fext=.jsp&c_id=nyy (September 29, 2011).

91 Rick Reilly, "A Gentleman in a Pinstripe Suit," *Sports Illustrated*, July 12, 2004, 156.

91 Katie Couric and Alex Rodriguez, quoted in "A-Rod: I've Never Used Steroids," *cbsnews.com*, June 12, 2009, http://www.cbsnews.com/

stories/2007/12/13/60minutes/main3617425.shtml (September 29, 2011).

91   Cynthia Rodriguez, quoted in "A-Rod's Wife Files for Divorce, Alleges Infidelity, 'Other Marital Misconduct,'" *ESPN.com*, July 7, 2008, http://sports.espn.go.com/mlb/news/story?id=3475674 (September 30, 2011).

92   Alex Rodriguez, quoted in "Rodriguez Admits, Regrets Use of PEDs," *ESPN.com*, February 10, 2009, http://sports.espn.go.com/mlb/news/story?id=3894847 (October 3, 2011).

92   Alex Rodriguez, quoted in "Rodriguez Hits the Ground Swinging," *nytimes.com*, May 8, 2009, http://www.nytimes.com/2009/05/09/sports/baseball/09yankees.html (September 30, 2011).

94   Alex Rodriguez, quoted in "Yankees Win 27th World Series Crown," *foxnews.com*, November 5, 2009, http://www.foxnews.com/us/2009/11/05/yankees-win-th-world-series-crown/ (October 3, 2011).

95   Cameron Diaz, quoted in "Cameron Diaz: Woman on Top," *harpersbazaar.com*, July 7, 2010, http://www.harpersbazaar.com/magazine/cover/cameron-diaz-interview-0810 (October 3, 2011).

97   Alex Rodriguez, quoted in "Yankees Alex Rodriguez Hits 600th Career Home Run," *usatoday.com*, August 4, 2010, http://content.usatoday.com/communities/dailypitch/post/2010/08/a-rod/1 (October 4, 2011).

98   Alex Rodriguez, quoted in "Deep in Texas, Only Rangers Had Heart," *ESPN.com*, October 23, 2010, http://sports.espn.go.com/new-york/mlb/columns/story?columnist=oconnor_ian&id=5716297 (October 4, 2011).

99   Alex Rodriguez quoted in "Rodriguez, with Leaner Physique and Healed Hip, Has Renewed Focus," *nytimes.com*, February 21, 2011, http://www.nytimes.com/2011/02/22/sports/baseball/22yankees.html (October 4, 2011).

99   Alex Rodriguez, quoted in "Yankees Lose to Tigers: Alex Rodriguez, Derek Jeter, and Jorge Posada Come Up Short in the ALDS," *huffingtonpost.com*, October 7, 2011, http://www.huffingtonpost.com/2011/10/07/yankees-arod-cano-posada-lose-tigers-mlb_n_999763.html (October 7, 2011).

99   Rodriguez and Brown, *Hit a Grand Slam!*, 35.

SELECTED BIBLIOGRAPHY

Books

Bradley, Michael. *Alex Rodriguez*. New York: Benchmark Books, 2005.

Christopher, Matt. *On the Field with . . . Alex Rodriguez*. New York: Little, Brown and Co., 2002.

Fitzgerald, James. *A-Rod: Major League Hero*. New York: Penguin Group, 2004.

Roberts, Selena. *A-Rod: The Many Lives of Alex Rodriguez*. New York: HarperCollins Publishers, 2010.

Torre, Joe and Tom Verducci. *The Yankee Years*. New York: Random House, 2010.

Selected Newspaper and Magazine Articles

Anthony, Mike. "Satisfying Turn for A-Rod; Puts to Rest Nightmares of First Season with Yankees." *Hartford (CT) Courant*, October 2, 2005.

Blum, Ronald. "Rodriguez Beats Ortiz to Win Second MVP in Three Seasons." Associated Press, November 14, 2005.

Cafardo, Nick. "A-Rod Introduced to Rivalry." *Boston Globe*, April 17, 2004.

Costello, Brian. "My Bad! A-Rod Apologized to Coaching Staff Following Game Five." *New York Post*, October 13, 2005.

Curry, Jack. "Rodriguez Is Haunted by Yanks' Collapse." *New York Times*, November 14, 2004.

De Luca, Chris. "Alex in Wonderland." *Chicago Sun-Times*, April 8, 2004.

Gonzales, Mark. "City Slicker; A-Rod Slowly Warms to a New York State of Mind." *Arizona Republic*, June 15, 2004.

O'Brien, Kathleen. "A-Rod Turns into A-Clod in ALCS." *Fort Worth Star-Telegram*, October 22, 2004.

Reilly, Rick. "A Gentleman in a Pinstripe Suit." *Sports Illustrated*, July 12, 2004.

FURTHER READING AND WEBSITES

Books

Greenberg, Keith Elliot. *Derek Jeter: Spectacular Shortstop*. Minneapolis: Twenty-First Century Books, 2011.

Kennedy, Mike, and Mark Stewart. *Long Ball: The Legend and Lore of the Home Run*. Minneapolis: Millbrook Press, 2006.

Krantz, Les. *Yankees Classics: World Series Magic from the Bronx Bombers, 1921 to Today*. Minneapolis: MVP Books, 2010.

Websites

AROD.com
http://www.arod.com
A-Rod's official site includes news headlines, stats, a photo gallery, a journal, and more.

Baseball-Reference.com
http://www.baseball-reference.com/r/rodrial01.shtml
This site includes A-Rod's complete batting and fielding statistics, awards he's won, and comparisons to other players.

ESPN.com
http://sports.espn.go.com/mlb/players/profile?statsId=5275
The sports channel site offers stats, scouting report information, and articles on the Yankee third baseman.

New York Yankees: The Official Site
http://www.yankees.com
This site is a great resource for everything you want to know about A-Rod's team.

INDEX

PHOTO ACKNOWLEDGMENTS

The images in this book are used with the permission of: © Robert Hanashiro/USA TODAY, pp. 1, 27, 69, 93, 95; © Jim McIsaac/Getty Images, pp. 3, 14, 21, 28, 35, 42, 53, 64, 72, 78, 96, 98; AP Photo/Morry Gash, pp. 4, 5; © Peter Keegan/Hulton Archive/ Getty Images, p. 7; © Eileen Blass/USA TODAY, p. 9 (bottom); © USA TODAY, p. 13; © David Bergman/CORBIS, p. 16; Seth Poppel Yearbook Library, pp. 19 (bottom), 22, 23; © David Bruneau/USA TODAY, pp. 20, 24; © Diamond Images/Getty Images, p. 26; AP Photo/Marta Lavandier, p. 30; AP Photo/Gary Stewart, p. 32; AP Photo/Osamu Honda, p. 33; © Stephen Dunn/Getty Images, pp. 40, 74; © Jonathan Daniel/Allsport/ Getty Images, p. 41; AP Photo/Michael Caulfield, p. 46; AP Photo/Linda Radin, p. 48; © H. Darr Beiser/USA TODAY, p. 49; © Brian Bahr/Getty Images, p. 50; AP Photo/Tony Gutierrez, p. 54; © Mike Enright/AFP/Getty Images, p. 56; AP Photo/John Froschauer, p. 58; © Linda Cataffo/NY Daily News Archive via Getty Images, pp. 61, 84; © Gary Barber/Allsport/Getty Images, p. 63; © Jeff Gross/Allsport/Getty Images, p. 66; © Dan Levine/AFP/Getty Images, p. 68; AP Photo/Mary Altaffer, p. 76; © Robert Deutsch/ USA TODAY, pp. 80, 87; AP Photo/Amy Sancetta, p. 83 (top); © Jonathan Daniel/Getty Images, p. 85; © Jay Gula/Getty Images, p. 88; © Chris McGrath/Getty Images, p. 94; AP Photo/Victor Calvo, p. 99.

Front cover: © Jim McIsaac/Getty Images.

Back cover: © Robert Deutsch/USA TODAY.

Main body text set in USA TODAY Roman Regular 10.5/15.

ABOUT THE AUTHOR

Serena Kappes is the author of two biographies for the Sports Heroes and Legends series, *Alex Rodriguez* and *Hank Aaron*. She is currently the editorial director for iVillage.com's Entertainment channel.